WA 1133647 1

This book is due for return on or before the last date shown below.

-4. MAR. 1991

D1513790

Don Gresswell Ltd., London, N.21 Cat. No. 1207

1979
The Cobden Trust
MIND

362.74
TAY

This book is dedicated to the memory of John Barter, whose particular genius was to inspire and encourage the work of others. John was a founding father of the campaign for children's rights in this country. As a member of NCCL's Children's Rights Committee over a decade ago, he helped many of us to recognise that a child's welfare could not be separated from his rights and liberties. As Deputy Director of MIND he was instrumental in translating that recognition into action, both within MIND and with other organisations in the field. John was a modest and quiet man whose influence was more often felt than seen.

Copyright © The Cobden Trust and MIND (National Association for Mental Health) 1980

ISBN 0 900137 13 4 (cloth) 0 900137 14 2 (paper)

PRINTED IN GREAT BRITAIN
by the Russell Press Ltd, Nottingham.

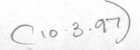
(10·3·97)

Contents

1. **Introduction**   7

2. **From Home to Institution: The Processing of Children**
   a. Why Children Go into Care   12
   b. Social Workers, Courts and Care Orders   22
   c. Representation of Children in Juvenile Courts   33
   d. Out of Care and Out of Court   37
   e. Perceptions of the Juvenile Court   42

3. **Within the Institution**
   a. Observation and Assessment   45
   b. Community Homes   49
   c. Special Schools, Mental Hospitals, Behavioural Units   54
   d. Detention Centres   62
   e. Borstals   64
   f. Means of Control: Prison: Secure Units: Drugs   71

4. **Conclusion and Recommendations**
   a. Standards for Juvenile Justice   85
   b. Grounds for Intervention   87
   c. Rights in Institutions   88
   d. Some Specific and Immediate Recommendations   90

5. **List of Relevant Organisations**   94

6. **Bibliography**   95

   Appendix: Legal Proceedings which lead to the
   Care or Custody of Children   98

Acknowledgements

We would like to thank a number of people who have given us help and advice during the preparation of this book: Robert Adams, Felix Fernando, Larry Gostin, Mary Jobbins, Tessa Jowell, Peter McKelvie, Ann Shearer, Pat Waterman, the members of the MIND Child Advocacy Panel and the following organisations: Justice for Children, Family Rights Group, National Childrens Bureau, Voice of the Child in Care. We must especially thank Norman Tutt, Professor of Applied Social Studies at the University of Lancaster for his critical comments upon the original manuscript. We are also grateful to Patricia Hewitt (National Council for Civil Liberties) and Tony Smythe (National Association for Mental Health) for their initial interest in the book and for their positive encouragement while it was being written.

We would like to make it clear that none of the above mentioned is in any way responsible for errors of fact or judgement within the text, and also make plain that the co-publication of the book by MIND and the Cobden Trust does not mean that either organisation is in necessary agreement with the specific recommendations which are made in the final section.

Finally, we should mention that the section on Borstal in this volume, although in accordance with the authors' views, was not in fact written by them, but by two workers within the system who at present wish to remain anonymous.

Preface

History will show whether or not the International Year of the Child, 1979, made any permanent, positive impact on the life and prospects of children and young people. It certainly provided the impetus for collaboration between the civil liberties and mental health movements with the result that we are jointly publishing this unique and profoundly disturbing study on what the authors conclusively show to be our flawed system of juvenile justice. We are deeply grateful to Laurie Taylor, Ron Lacey and Denis Bracken for their speed, energy and insight in assembling the material (material that was available for anyone who chose to look, though often buried in obscure academic and specialist journals), producing both a coherent analysis and an unanswerable case for urgent reform.

The evidence presented suggests that the child care system is built on confusion which has accumulated and been reinforced by layers of legislation, conflicts of practice and goals, and a steadfast refusal to face facts. Notions of care, treatment and protection have tended to suffocate the principles of natural justice. Perceptions of how the system works and what it is for vary alarmingly among those who can assign people into it and those who provide it and these seem to bear very little relation to how the consumers, children and their families experience the end product: indeed, it is the consumers who on this evidence seem to be most realistic. Objectively, the consumers of the care system are likely to be poor and disadvantaged. Admission into the care system may be a recipe for personal destruction. Some survive, but others embark upon a career of institutional living, perpetual supervision, dependency and delinquency.

When a society makes major mistakes there is a tendency to look around for someone to blame. As the authors show children and their parents are often blamed for events beyond their control. A careless reading of this book may cause some to attribute blame to the people who provide the care. This would be unproductive and unfair. From inside a system it is not easy to change it or even to see what is wrong with it. Residential workers, many of the under-trained and many more under-paid, are always under the pressure of meeting demands and expectations beyond their resources. They are often made to feel that they are expected to get on with the job regardless of the cost to themselves with the minimum of help and understanding from outside. If nothing goes visibly wrong they are forgotten. If their failures are noticed they are targets for criticism, usually from the uninformed. There is, in fact a great deal

5

of expertise and dedication around. It could be mobilised if the recommendations of this book were accepted.

Our greatest fear is that those in a position to implement the changes argued for in this book will ignore it because of the apparent enormity of the task or because, in a time of economic retrenchment, it would be inexpedient to acknowledge past failure and to move in a direction which conflicts with a rising climate of repression. Our organisations will do what they can to broadcast the facts and bring pressure to bear on the policy makers. We hope that the victims of the care system will be more wary of the experts, more confident about insisting on choice, and more outspoken.

We hope that those who deliver the services will debate the issues raised and communicate their concerns to the public, the planners and their colleagues. Total solutions will remain illusive and there are many issues which deserve further exploration. Nevertheless, the process of change must start and some radical reforms introduced without delay. It is unthinkable that we should continue to build on the errors of the past until the whole system explodes or becomes totally unworkable. The International Year of the Child had inevitably produced its crop of well-meaning platitudes. Where justice for children is concerned, we have an obligation to act.

Tony Smythe
Director, MIND
Patricia Hewitt
Trustee, Cobden Trust
December 1979

1

Introduction

This book draws attention to the grossly unsatisfactory manner in which our courts and institutions handle difficult, disturbed and deprived children. It provides evidence that injustice, hypocrisy, and the denial of human rights, occur within every part of the present system.

It is hardly an attack on current policy in that one would be pressed to find anything resembling a policy within existing practise. Half-realised ideas from the 1969 Children and Young Persons Act jostle uneasily with traditional disciplinarian principles and bits and pieces of political expediency.

Nothing perhaps provides a more dramatic illustration of the barrenness of of our present situation than the recent announcements (October 1979) on the treatment of juveniles made by Conservative Home Secretary William Whitelaw.* First, he announced, on an *experimental* basis, two new detention centres with especially strict regimes to deal with young offenders even though just such an experiment was tried in the 1950s and proved unsuccessful. Then secondly, in deference to recent demands by magistrates, he allowed an adjustment to the 1969 Children and Young Persons Act, so that magistrates may have the power to insist that children on a care order go directly into residential care. All this despite evidence of the dramatic increases in the use of such institutions in recent years, evidence of the inefficacy of such a policy, and evidence that those children who at the moment go home rather than into a community home or assessment centre as a result of a care order, do so not because of social workers' liberality but simply because of the non-availability of resources. (Resources incidentally which are now being even further reduced as a result of local authority spending cuts.)

The principal subjects of this book are children who for a variety of reasons have been removed from their home and community and placed in one of a number of different institutions often on the grounds that this in one way or another is 'in their best interests'. The number of such children as the table below indicates is very high, nearly twice as high, for example, as the number of adult prisoners in England and Wales.

*This is hardly a political note: there is nothing much in the Labour Party's performance in this area which might count as a positive alternative to Mr Whitelaw's policy.

Children in Institutions (Approximate figures)

	1977/78
Children in Care (Community Homes, Assessment Centres, etc.)	34,000
Special Schools (Educationally Sub Normal, Maladjusted, Physically and Mentally Handicapped)	28,000
Hospitals for Mental Illness and Mental Handicap	4,600
Detention Centres (Under 17)	1,900
Borstals (Under 17)	2,000
Total	70,500

The initial concern about many of the children behind these statistics came from Ron Lacey's experience as a social work advocate for MIND. About five years ago this organisation started a legal and welfare rights service for mental patients. From the beginning, however, MIND found itself approached by lawyers, parents and children asking for advice and help over cases involving care and other proceedings in the juvenile court. As the volume of these requests increased, it became clear that many of the issues which arose in the work with, and for, the mentally ill were directly comparable to those affecting children. The child in law seemed to have much in common with the mentally ill adult.

Working for MIND as a child advocate typically involved the preparation of arguments which might refute those presented by professional social workers who claimed to be operating in the 'best interests of the child'. Over a period of five years, approximately one hundred cases have been dealt with, and much of the material and discussion in this book derives from these case files. In addition we have received considerable help from a number of 'inside sources' who obviously do not wish to be specifically identified. The involvement of the Cobden Trust in the enterprise is a natural consequence of that organisation's association with the National Council for Civil Liberties, and thereby with the questions about the deprivation of liberty involved in the removal of children from their homes. The basic argument of this book is that the most promising way to remedy some of the hypocrisies and ambiguities which regularly recur in these cases is through a strong injection of notions of natural justice into present procedures, and through the development of a charter of children's rights.

Although last year was the International Year of the Child there has been little informed discussion of such matters. It is true that there were mentions of children's rights during the International Year, but a great deal of this either took a rather vacuous turn with references to such matters as the child's right to have a good home life (hands up all those against that one!), or, alternatively, the issue was used by special interest groups to promote their own ends. The trick is quite simple. It involves transposing your own wishes into the language of other's rights. You're in the business of selling organised religion? Fine. All you need to do is campaign hard on the issue of child's spiritual rights! Baby food? Then how about the child's right to appropriate nutrition?

A second, and we believe, more important justification for our emphasis upon natural justice and rights for the child, is that it provides a necessary antidote to the usual debate in this country about juvenile justice. Much of this

8

debate seems to have involved the search for an ideal solution to the problem of deprived and delinquent children. Ten years ago, in the eyes of those who supported the 1969 Children and Young Person's Act and the discussion which preceded it, the panacea was the introduction of a treatment and rehabilitative ethic into areas which had previously seemed primarily punitive or repressive. Lengthy debate about the deficiencies of the Act (which student of social work in the last five years has not had to write an essay on the conflict between treatment and the punitive elements in the juvenile court?) now seems to be culminating in a call, from both left and right, for a return to notions of responsibility and punishment. At all times new views on juvenile justice are presented as an improvement on the present state of affairs, as evidence that some progress is being made, that previous failures are being corrected.

There is an element of *naïveté* in all this debate — a failure to recognise that there is nothing intrinsically radical or reactionary about punitive or rehabilitative models of juvenile justice. Both are open to serious abuse, to violations of basic rights and of natural justice. Indeed, as we have seen with the operation of the 1969 Act, such abuses may well be minimised or ignored for long periods of time if there is an ideological blanket under which they may be concealed. We believe that our concentration upon natural justice in the processing and institutionalisation of children provides an important bench-mark against which the relative 'progressiveness' of proposed reforms may be set. Much of our book, for example, documents the ways in which the apparent liberality of the 1969 Act was fundamentally undermined by its central assumption — the idea that there were those who knew what was best for the child — in fact knew so well, that there was no requirement that they produce evidence to support their claims.

Natural justice is not of course some absolute concept which can be carried into each and every situation as a kind of measuring rod. Our own use of the term will become clearer throughout the following chapters but at this point we may say that it minimally entails the right of any child or his/her parents or their representatives, to bring evidence to show that any particular course of action proposed by legal or social work authorities in 'the interests of the child' — e.g. allocation of a care order, commitment to a community home or special school — is not in fact in those interests. It also requires that access to necessary information in such cases is available to all parties and that there are adequate opportunities for appeal.

In addition to invoking the concept of natural justice in connection with the processing of juveniles, we also raise the question of rights in regard to the day-to-day existence of the child in any institution to which he/she may eventually be committed.

Although much of what follows can be read as an oblique or direct attack upon current social work practise, it should be emphasised that this is not because we subscribe to some crude 'self-help' theory of society. It is simply because any concern with natural justice and rights in this area entails confrontation with *present* social work ideology and practise. We do not believe that this contradiction between rights and welfare is a necessary one, but rather a product of a particular view of the relationship between the two, and would therefore be disappointed if our book were to be read as another contribution to the 'knock-

9

the-social-worker' literature. Indeed, we would argue that the articulation of clear standards of justice and the acknowledgement of specific children's rights would do much to resolve the recurrent predicaments which are faced by social workers and residential staff. For example, a conscientious social worker's concern about the correctness of recommending institutional treatment for a particular child would be considerably assuaged by the knowledge that alternative suggestions had been adequately aired in court by child, parent, lawyer or expert witness. And humanitarian staff in residential establishments faced with dilemmas about the use of drugs to control their charges, or about the need to resort to secure accommodation for disciplinary purposes or about the lack of necessary resources, would be similarly assisted by being able to refer to a strict set of children's rights which laid down strict material standards and explicitly outlawed certain practises, or provided an opportunity for them to be independently evaluated.

Neither would we like our book to be regarded as a plea for legalism. It is perfectly true that a dose of 'due process' might do much to cure that unhealthy mixture of collusion, confidentiality and professional expertise which at present does so much to lend an arbitrary, uneven, or even downright conspiratorial aspect to juvenile proceedings. But the danger of promoting 'legality' for its own sake is that attention then becomes entirely focused upon the formal 'correctness' of procedural aspects of justice. More substantive concerns about whether or not children should be punished for their minor offences, or whether or not they should be institutionalised without any investigation of the comparative merits of home and institution, or whether their material conditions or age can be taken into account when determining an appropriate sentence, are pushed to one side. Of course legality has been used to further ideas of natural justice and rights but to regard this as somehow an emergent property of legaility is hopelessly misleading. As one writer has recently observed:

'One cannot simply take legality and see it in isolation from the other social factors upon which it is founded . . . its usefulness as a concept to any group in society depends on the context in which it operates.' (Prosser 1977)

All of which means that our book is a blend of demands for procedural change (e.g. representation in court, visibility of social enquiry reports) and substantive reform (e.g. the abolition of secure units and assessment centres). We repeat that we have not attempted to cover every aspect of juvenile justice — the role of community service orders and intermediate treatment are significant omissions — but have rather concentrated on those areas in which arise the most serious questions about natural justice and rights.

As a final precaution against the possibility of this book being read as an attack upon the social work profession, the magistracy, or the staff of residential institutions, rather than as a proposed corrective to their present practices, we list below the questions about natural justice and rights which we will be addressing to members of these groups at different stages of the text.

1. Is any coercive intervention which is proposed genuinely in the 'best interests of the child'?
2. To what extent is such intervention based not upon the personal characteristics of child or parent but upon socio-economic circumstances beyond their control?

3. What opportunities exist for the child and for his/her parent or representatives to question the decision which is allegedly made in his/her 'best interests'?

4. To what extent are those who propose intervention required to justify their claims by balancing the child's present situation against the likely results of institutionalisation?

5. In the event of children being removed from home and community to institution, what provisions exist for the maintenance of the basic rights they would enjoy outside that institution?

The unsatisfactory nature of the answers which can be given to such questions in the present system of child care and juvenile justice, leads us to make a large number of specific recommendations. Most of these appear throughout the text, but we thought it helpful to formulate them more explicitly and systematically in a final chapter.

January 1980.

2
From Home to Institution: The Processing of Children

2a. Why Children Go Into Care

As the main theme of this book is the intervention which is made by various authorities into children's lives, and the consequences of that intervention, it is appropriate to begin with a consideration of 'care'. On 31 March 1977 there were 101,000 children in care in England and Wales. About one-third of these were living in community homes and community schools (approved schools), or in assessment centres awaiting allocation, another third were boarded out with foster parents, the remainder were still at home. All were united by the fact that the local authority had for varying periods of time and with varying degrees of compulsion assumed responsibility for their health and welfare on the grounds that such matters could no longer be adequately attended to in the child's own family and community.

When we look for more specific reasons for a child being in 'care' we are confronted with a range of conditions arising from several different pieces of legislation. (A special appendix to this book summarises these possibilities.) For example we find that 13,000 children are in care as a result of Section 1 of the 1948 Act in that they have 'been deserted by parent, (with) other parent unable to provide care'. Another 1,500 children are in community homes and assessment centres as a result of the operation of Section 1 (2) (4) of the 1969 Act, in that they 'are regarded as being exposed to moral danger'. Nearly 19,000 children find themselves in care as a result of the operation of the 'offence condition' of the 1969 Children and Young Persons Act. That is they are children who have been brought before the juvenile court as a result of committing an offence, and then, on the basis of a variety of reports, been found to be in need of care and control. It is unfortunate that the characteristics of this group are often assumed to be those common to all care cases, for although the proportion of children in care as a result of this condition is relatively small (under 20%) there is a frequent tendency to assume that most children placed in care have committed some form of criminal offence, even to believe that most of them have deserved to be sent away from home. (The readiness of children themselves to perpetuate this belief is discussed in our chapter on community homes.)

In fact the majority of the 82,100 who make up the 'non-offence' children in care have played no part whatsoever in their eventual disposition. They are there

12

because, it has been argued, in a variety of ways, that 'care' is in their own 'best interests'. In many cases, there is no doubt about these best interests being served, about the beneficial effects of such local authority intervention. Clearly children whose parents have died, or deserted them, or severely brutalised them, hardly have their best interests served by remaining at home. But a disturbing feature of the present system is that the credibility which social workers and local authorities gain from such necessary interventions can become unreasonably extended to cover other interventions made for much less clear reasons. The particular danger is that benevolent and individualistic notions of 'care' (the desolate child being helped by paternal local authority) can disguise the fact that many children who go into 'care' go not because of purely private familial reasons but actually as a result of official policy. And ironically, the practical implementation of that policy is often the responsibility of none other than the 'benevolent' local authority.

Perhaps the easiest way in which to expose this aspect of 'care' is by considering those children who have been *received into care* rather than *committed* to care. The former category which accounts for 47,600 of the total of 101,000 is frequently referred to as 'voluntary' in that such children are presumed to have been taken into care by the local authority at the request of their parents or guardians, as distinct from the 48,100 children who are in care on the initiative of the local authority.

'Received into care' implies that the parent have made a positive choice to put their child into care, and indeed the figures showing that approximately 55% of those placed in care under the 1948 Act leave care after periods of eight weeks or less lends support to such a conclusion, as does the information that the majority of such children were in care on the grounds that their parents or guardians suffered from a temporary incapacity to care for them, such as illness, or confinement. However, a closer examination of this category by researchers has revealed that the notion of care as a chosen option may apply to fewer children than usually supposed.

Robert Holman and others have shown, for example, that poverty (hardly a characteristic 'voluntarily' adopted by parents) is a major factor in determining whether a child is received into care or not. Holman observes that children received into care appear to come in disproportionate numbers from geographical areas of social deprivation. Thus the local authorities with the highest rates are those inner London boroughs with extensive poverty, overcrowding and inadequate housing conditions. Tower Hamlets, Kensington and Chelsea, Hammersmith and Camden annually take into care between 20 and 28 children per 1,000 children under 18. Outside London too the highest numbers occur in depressed urban areas — Manchester, Newcastle, Bradford, Oldham.

A similar pattern obtains *within* single local authorities. Over two-thirds of the children in the care of the Portsmouth authority in March 1974 were drawn from just five of the city's sixteen wards. These five tended to be those with the highest proportion of unskilled manual workers, lone parents and inadequate housing. Holman concludes 'the children of the poor are more likely than other sections of the population to be taken away from their parents'. (Holman 1976: the significance of these factors is further confirmed in a recent study carried out by the Harlesden Community Project in the London Borough of Brent.)

A further reservation about the 'voluntary' status of those children received into care is provided by the 'homeless' category. The DHSS figures for the year ending 31 March 1977 refer to 2,000 children being in care and 1,200 received into care on the grounds of 'Family Homeless (eviction or other cause)'. This is an interesting revelation in that homelessness is not referred to in the Act as grounds for reception into care, and in that it may even be unlawful to receive a child into care on these grounds. Section 1 of the Children and Young Persons Act 1969 imposes a duty on local authorities 'to make available such advice, guidance and assistance as may promote the welfare of children by diminishing the need to receive children into care or to keep them in care under the Children Act 1948 . . .' This clearly suggests that local authorities are required to prevent children from being received into care by providing such 'assistance' as priority rehousing, help with rent arrears, or by arranging for families to be temporarily accommodated in hotels. However, under pressure from the Government's policy to reduce public expenditure, the tide is actually turning the other way. A number of local authorities have announced their intention to receive into care the children of families who have been determined by their housing officials to be 'intentionally homeless'. Some authorities are going further and suggesting that if such parents cannot be persuaded to separate from their children, then place of safety orders will be obtained (section 28 (2), Children and Young Persons Act 1969) to facilitate the enforced removal into care of those children.

In a recent article a Wandsworth Labour opposition councillor is quoted as expressing her concern that the social services would seek place of safety orders on children whose parents would not agree to their being received into care. The fact that this councillor is the former chairperson of the social services committee strongly suggests that she knows social services well enough to predict with some accuracy their likely response to the situation (*Community Care*, 2 August 1979).

The significance of this and other cases was underlined recently in the editorial of a social work journal:

When is an ethic not an ethic? Perhaps when it's applied by the social work profession. In recent weeks we have documented a growing number of instances where local authority housing departments seem to be effectively engineering the principles of social services departments. In Maidstone, Bradford, Wandsworth and more recently in Dorset and Redbridge . . . Housing departments have interpreted the 1977 Homeless Persons Act in such a way as to leave families with children without a roof over their heads. Often this has involved judgements, sometimes dubious, sometimes downright harsh, as to whether the family made themselves homeless intentionally. (*Community Care*, 30 August 1979).

Certainly the category of 'intentionally homeless' can easily become stretched to include those families who spend their allowances on food, clothes and comforts for their children and themselves to the extent that they amass rent arrears, those containing battered wives who leave home to avoid brutality, those families who uproot themselves in an attempt to find employment.

The term voluntary when applied to a person's decisions and actions implies the exercise of positive choices between realistic alternatives. Thus a mother may choose to take her baby to hospital with her rather than place her in care, or a lone father may choose to stay at home to care for his child if financial support is offered, or a single mother may choose to keep her child if day care is available, etc. Such choices on the part of parents depend on the provision of facilities in the community and on the priority given by social workers and others to the preventative duties of local authorities. In the situations we have described, local authority practices have effectively frustrated the possibility of a real choice. Indeed their recent activities in relation to the children of homeless families suggests that it is they, rather than parents, who exercise the real choice, in that present law allows them considerable discretion as to how, when and indeed whether, they discharge their statutory duties to prevent the need for children to be received into care.

An even more ominous aspect of this tendency to regard 'reception into care' as evidence of personal shortcomings rather than public derelictions, is that such a philosophy actually appears to influence major policy decisions. As Robert Holman has argued the whole direction of social policy in recent years has not been towards providing the financial and practical resources (e.g. child care facilities) which might do something to relieve the material and practical difficulties of poor parents, but has rather gone along with the pathological argument which stresses the psychological shortcomings of the home. So, for example, the Children Act (1975) has nothing whatsoever to say about day care amenities, housing or income maintenance, but instead 'concentrates exclusively on facilitating the removal of children from their families and on reducing the rights of natural parents'. (Holman, 1976)

In the circumstances we have described it seems, therefore, both irrelevant and misleading to make too clearcut a distinction between those cases in which children were 'received' into care because their own parents decided that they could no longer cope with circumstances beyond their control, and those cases involving similar circumstances, but in which the local authority took the initiative and resorted to 'committal'. The political significance of being able to

---

The *National Child Development Study* results confirm that even children who come into short-term care, ostensibly because of their mother's confinement, tend to belong to socially disadvantaged families. Earlier findings have also shown that large families with low income, those where there is only one parent, or where there is physical or mental handicap, are at greater risk of disintegration, and that once a family is split up, reintegration may be difficult. The Needs of Children. Mai Kellmer Pringle, Hutchinson, London 1974.

---

stress the voluntariness of so many receptions into care is that it prompts local authorities, and perhaps more importantly parents and children themselves, to regard such cases as an admission of private failure rather than as a result of public policy. This is particularly relevant at the moment in that the present cut-backs in local authority provision for the more disadvantaged members of the community look likely to make the word 'voluntary' an ever more inappropriate description of 'reception' into care, than it is at present.

The affront to natural justice which occurs when parents are forced to ask local authorities to care for their children because such local authorities have failed to carry out their statutory duties may well be compounded by later actions which interfere with their chances of reclaiming such children. When a local authority has received a child it can in certain circumstances, without recourse to the courts, assume the parental rights over a child in respect of one or both of his parent, under the provisions of section 2 of the Children Act 1948. This can and is often done through a relatively simple procedure whereby a social worker writes a report recommending that these rights be assumed. The local authority is obliged to notify a parent of its intention and to advise them that they can lodge an objection in the juvenile court, in which circumstances the local authority is obliged to make a case before the magistrates. In this way, the burden of bringing the matter before the court is left with the parent, who may be poor, inarticulate and intimidated by the prospect of engaging in legal proceedings against the local authority. The fact that the ultimate responsibility for the decision rests with the elected members rather than the officers of the authority is supposed, in theory, to provide a check against the possibility that the social worker may exceed or abuse his legal powers. However, in practice the elected members provide little more than a rubber stamp for the decisions of their officers. One of the authors was recently informed by Camden's Chairman of Social Services, that there had not been one occasion when the elected members had declined to assume parental rights and powers when it had been recommended by its officers, during the preceding five years. He, himself could recall no occasion during his 10 years in local authority social work in three different authorities, where a recommendation to assume a parent's rights and powers was not agreed to by a social services committee.

The extent to which these powers are used can be judged by the 1977 statistics, which reveal that 16,200 children, that is to say a little under a third of the total number of children who had originally been received into care, were in care subject to a resolution under the provisions of section 2 of the 1948 Act. (*Children in Care in England and Wales,* 1977, paragraph 5, p.6.) This represented an increase on the previous year's total of 12.9%. This is, of course, a crude statistic in that many of these children's parents may be dead, or have completely abandoned them. Equally in the case of other children there will be substantial grounds which make it necessary to their welfare that the rights and powers of their parents are taken over by a local authority. However, given the numbers involved and taking into account the reasons and circumstances under which they may have first entered the care system, such figures make the initial use of the word 'voluntary' seem even less appropriate. It should also be borne in mind that parents whose children remain in care under the 1948 Act for more than six months, cannot discharge their children from care without local authority approval. Such a parent must give 28 days notice to the local authority of his/her intention to discharge the child. Having been given this notice, a local authority can if it desires institute the procedures to assume the parent's rights and powers or make an application for the child to be made a ward of court. Thus it is possible within the present law for a protesting child to be held from a willing parent if in the opinion of the local authority his/her welfare demands

> # Expenditure on Children in Care and as a percentage of Local Authority Budgets
>
> Total Gross expenditure by local authorities for the fiscal year
> 1975/1976 £13,256,000,000
> Expenditures by local authorities for Personal Social Services for year
> ending 31 March 1976 £867,739,000
> Total Gross expenditure by local authorities on children in care for year
> ending 31 March 1976 £150,767,000
> England £143,695,000
> Wales £7,072,000
> Expenditures on personal social services amounts to 6.54% of the total
> gross expenditure by local authorities in the year 75-76.
> Expenditures on children in care amounts to 1.14% of the total gross
> expenditure by local authorities in the year 75-76.
> Expenditures on children in care amounts to 17.37% of the amount spent
> by local authorities on personal social services in the year 75-76.
> Increase in expenditure on children in care between 75-76 and 76-77
> is 19.19%.

it. In practice, this means that the child who enters care 'voluntarily' under the 1948 Act. and whose parents' rights are removed under Section 2 is even more isolated from the courts than the child who has been committed to care under other children's legislation. It is, for example, possible for the latter child through his parent or other person with a proper interest, to seek directions from the High Court, limiting the discretions exercised by the local authority in caring for him.

Committed to care

We will deal at length in a later section with those large numbers of commitals to care (care orders) in which an offence is involved. Here, however, we will concentrate upon two other examples of care orders which raise important questions of natural justice. These are Sections 1 (2) (c) and 1 (2) (e) of the 1969 Children and Young Persons Act.

Section 1 (2) (c) allows a care order to be made if the court before which the child or young person is brought is satisfied that he/she is exposed to moral danger. The number in care under this provision in 1977 was 1500. Although the statistics do not make any distinctions within this category, our experience clearly suggests that those most likely to be committed to care under this provision are girls deemed to be 'promiscuous'. Boys are rarely if ever thus described, and so that in practice this provision refers to girls who engage in sexual intercourse under the present age of consent of 16.

The relative frequency with which sexual intercourse under the age of 16 now occurs has, of course, led to many claims that the present age of consent is totally unrealistic and requires reform. For example, a working party set up by

Children in care of local authorities: Circumstances in which children came into care
Years ended 31 March 1977

	England 1971	1972	1973	1974	1975	Thousands 1976
Admission to the care of local authorities	68.0	61.1	60.8	60.3	59.1	61.1
Abandoned or lost	0.7	0.8	1.0	1.0	1.2	1.0
Death of, or deserted by, mother: father unable to care	6.0	5.5	5.2	5.0	4.1	3.5
Incapacity of parent or guardian:-						
– confinement	5.1	4.3	3.7	2.7	2.3	1.9
– short-term illness	15.5	15.2	15.0	13.4	12.2	11.9
– long-term illness or incapacity	1.3	1.0	1.0	1.0	0.7	0.8
Child illegitimate – mother unable to provide	2.3	1.9	1.9	1.8	1.7	1.6
Parent or guardian in prison or remanded in custody	1.0	0.9	0.9	0.9	0.8	0.9
Family homeless – through eviction	1.4	1.1	0.8	0.7	0.4	0.3
– through other cause	1.5	1.7	1.8	1.5	1.1	0.9
Unsatisfactory home conditions	3.0	3.4	4.2	4.5	4.6	5.0
Fit person orders – offenders[1]	6.7					
– non-offenders[1]						
Care orders made under:-						
Sections 1 (2), 7 (7), 15 (1), and 25 (1) or 26 (2) of the Children and Young Persons Act, 1969		9.1	8.9	9.6	10.8	11.5
Interim care orders or on remand to care[2]	6.2	9.9	9.4	9.8	10.0	11.1
Transitional provisions of the Children and Young Persons Act, 1969[2]	11.7					
Other reasons	5.6	6.3	7.0	8.4	9.2	10.8

1. On 1 January 1971 the power of the Courts to commit to approved school or to the care of a fit person was abolished and replaced by the power to commit to the care of a local authority. Children and young persons aged under 19 then subject to approved school orders, or to supervision after release from an approved school, were deemed from 1 January 1971 to be subject to care orders. On the same date the system of remand to a remand home was replaced by committal to care under an interim care order or remand to care.

2. Interim fit person orders (April-December 1970) or interim care orders or on remand to care (January-March 1971).

Children in care of local authorities: Reasons for children going out of care
Years ended 31 March 1977

Circumstances in which children went out of care (not including remand cases and those subject to interim orders)	England 1971	1972	1973	1974	1975	Thousands 1976
Total	46,853	48,676	49,097	48,118	45,605	48,294
Becoming self-supporting or care taken over by a parent, guardian, relative or friend	37,650	37,542	37,299	35,540	32,143	33,430
Adopted	1,716	1,555	1,431	1,491	1,429	1,456
Emigrated	27	29	52	140	95	74
Attained age of 18	4,235	5,584	6,000	6,050	6,285	7,230
Attained age of 19	118	491	622	712	836	683
Died	111	115	115	106	143	132
Other reasons	2,996	3,360	3,578	4,079	4,674	5,289

Source: Tables 7.16 and 7.17.

19

the National Council for One-Parent Families and the Community Development Trust has recently produced (September 1979) a report based on four years research which declares that the present age of consent is now out of touch with reality. The report recommends, not the lowering of the age of consent, but its abolition. But even without advocating such changes, it seems singularly unjust that a small group of female 'offenders' (whose 'derelictions' may well have become known to the authorities as a result of the family's other involvements with social welfare agencies) should be singled out for special attention in this way, especially as such attention may result in them spending many years undergoing 'treatment'. Similarly unjust is the application of this provision to homosexual activity.

Perhaps even more disturbing, at least in terms of the numbers affected by the provision, is the operation of Section 1 (2) (e) of the 1969 Act. This allows a care order to be made if the child is of compulsory school age within the meaning of the Education Act 1944, and is not receiving sufficient full-time education suitable to his/her age, ability or aptitude. In 1977, 4,300 children were in care as a result of this provision, largely on the grounds that they had persistently truanted. There are two principal reasons for concern about such figures. In the first place it seems highly unreasonable for courts to regard such persistent truancy as evidence of a personal need for care, without conducting any evaluation of the overall truancy rates in those schools from which the 'offenders' are absenting themselves. Figures are of course difficult to obtain in that headteachers have no wish to advertise the inability of their schools to maintain pupil commitment, but an analysis by one of the present authors of an area in which such provision had been frequently invoked indicated that the regular truancy rate among pupils over the age of 13 in two schools was approximately 30 per cent. Even more interesting was the finding that those reported by educational authorities for 'truancy' were more likely to be children who had attended irregularly and created 'trouble' than those who had simply absented themselves without explanation for long periods of time.

A second cause for concern in relation to this section of the Act is the court's unreadiness to hear any defence by the 'truant' which cites the inadequacy or the inappropriateness of the education he/she is required to receive, as grounds for this unreadiness to attend. This effectively insulates the education authority and its teaching staff from any blame for educational failure, and locates the dereliction within the personal characteristics of the truant — a further example of the transformation of a public issue into a private trouble.

It is interesting to see that this unilateral view of truancy has been recently challenged in certain areas of this country by social workers who are reluctant to take over the education authorities' problems by bringing regular truants before the courts. However, this small resistance may well be countered by recently announced police intentions to form 'truancy squads' which would round up absentees and bring them before the courts. Although objections have been raised to such practices on the grounds that truancy is not a criminal offence and therefore is no concern of the police, the evidence of a relationship between delinquency and truancy may well be enough to overcome such objections in the near future.

We believe that many of the present ambiguities which exist within the legislation relating to care might best be resolved by the adoption of a more rigorous set of 'grounds for intervention'. A possible set of such grounds is outlined in the final part of this book, but at this stage it seems worthwhile to translate some of the specific objections to intervention which we have raised in this section, into definite recommendations.

1. A child should not be received into care or committed to care, on the grounds that his/her parent or guardian is homeless, no matter how such homelessness might be caused.
2. A child should not be received into care or committed to the care of a local authority, simply or substantially on the grounds that his/her parent or guardian does not have the financial resources to meet his/her primary physical needs.
3. A child should not be received into care or committed to the care of a local authority, simply or substantially on the grounds that he/she does not attend school.
4. No child should be received into care or committed to the care of a local authority simply or substantially on the grounds that they have engaged in unlawful sexual intercourse or homosexual activity.

The 'Offence' Condition

We referred earlier to the proportion of children who found themselves in care (under 20% of the total care population) as a result of the operation of the 'offence' condition of the 1969 Act, which allows the juvenile court to make a care order when a young person has been found to be guilty of an offence (excluding homicide) and also to be in need of 'care and control'.

It is the operation of this section of the Act (and sometimes the very presence in the Act) which has probably occasioned the greatest number of practical and philosophical criticisms of our present system of juvenile justice. Many of these will be referred to in the different sections of this text but here we concentrate specifically upon the extent to which natural justice obtains in the committals to care which arise from the enforcement of the provisions.

For some time there has been a suspicion that the decision to issue a care order under this section has been related less to the actual need of the child for 'care and control' and rather more to the court's feeling that the institutional options which a care order may entail (assessment centre, community home) are a suitable 'sentence' for the offence under consideration. In other words the care criteria are being as carelessly applied as they were in some of the other care proceedings that we have described.

Confirmation of this suspicion has come from a variety of sources. Pat Cawson's study of 497 young people committed to care, for example, indicated that care orders were hardly being issued as a last resort, after all other alternatives had been tried and found wanting.

The results emphatically suggest that, in a large proportion of cases, committal to care for delinquency is being used as a first or early resort, not as a last resort. A third of the sample had apparently been committed to care without any attempt at non-residential solutions. (Cawson, 1978)

Further evidence of the courts' inappropriate use of the care order under the offence condition comes from David Thorpe and his fellow researchers at Lancaster University, who analysed the characteristics of 132 young offenders committed to residential care by one local authority. (Thorpe, Paley and Green, 1979.) In order to assess the need for such care, they asked in each case, 'Was the child a danger to himself or the community?' 'Does he have any special needs, educational, medical or otherwise which could only be met in an institution?' 'Is he without a home to go to — in that family pressures make life at home intolerable?' If any of these criteria were satisfied, then Thorpe *et al* allowed that residential care was necessary. Out of the 132 children considered only 13 satisfied one or more of the criteria: '119 (90%) did not require residential care, there being no reason why they should not live in the community.'

At the moment there are approximately 10,000 young offenders, held on care orders in community homes of various types. If Thorpe's findings hold for other local authorities, then approximately 9,000 of these children might have survived in the community without serious consequences for themselves or for those around them.

But even more alarming is the finding by Thorpe *et al* that of the 119 cases, one-third received a care order on their first court appearance, and that most of the offences committed by children in this group and in the whole sample were non-serious. (In all cases of theft, for example, the median figure of the value of the goods stolen was less than £10). It seems that in many instances young offenders subject to Section 7 (7) of the 1969 Act are likely to spend considerable periods of time in residential institutions whereas if similar offences had been committed by adults, imprisonment would have been highly unlikely (Thorpe *et al* 1979).

2b. Social Workers, Courts, and Care Orders

We have outlined several general reasons for concern about the present use of care orders in our existing system of child care and juvenile justice. We now need to examine the particular elements within the present system (the prevailing child care philosophy, the relative influence of social workers and magistrates) which combine to produce some of the unsatisfactory outcomes we have described.

Under English law the child enjoys very few of the rights taken for granted by adults under the principles of natural justice. The law's reference to the child's 'best interests', reflects the benevolent paternalism of its approach. Essentially, as far as the courts are concerned, the 'best interests' principle empowers social workers, psychologists, psychiatrists and others to define, on the basis of their opinions, what is good for the child. In this the law assumes that the 'experts' have at their disposal the means by which not only to *define* but also to *meet* the needs of a particular child who may be in 'moral danger', or 'whose proper health and development is being avoidably impaired' or who is 'beyond the control of his parent'. It does not require that the experts should substantiate their opinions or prove to the court that any course of action they propose will be more effective in promoting the best interests of the child than those taken by the parent, or by the child acting on his own behalf. Thus parents of children before the courts are often in the invidious position of having their capacity as parents measured against some unspecified ideal type. Or a child may find that his/her arguments against being committed to care are perceived as evidence of their need for treatment, as a sign, for example, that they have 'authority problems'.

Any adult appearing before a court expects to know fully the case which they have to answer, particularly in a matter in which their liberty is at stake. However, in care proceedings the rights of a parent and/or the liberty of the child will in most cases be decided on the basis of the contents of the *social enquiry report* which is prepared for the court's inspection by a probation officer, or more usually, in the case of younger people, by a social worker.

The social enquiry report is in many respects the cornerstone of the juvenile court. It is the element in the proceedings which has the most immediate reference to the 1969 Act. The duty for local authorities to provide information on children appearing in court was contained in the 1933 Children and Young Persons Act, but this was qualified by the phrase 'except in cases which appear to them to be of a trivial nature'. Section 9.1 of the 1969 Act is much stronger.

Now such reports (called 'social enquiry reports' on the recommendation of the 1962 Morrisson Committee) are required *unless* there is a positive reason for not providing them. And, of course, they have now acquired even more importance in that, if the intentions of the Act are being observed, it is highly unlikely that any case actually reaching the court will be of a minor nature.* In these circumstances it would seem a self-evident requirement of natural justice that such reports should be automatically available to the child, their legal representative and/or their parent prior to hearing. In fact under existing rules there is no absolute requirement that even a child's lawyer should receive copies of reports. And certainly there is no necessity that social enquiry reports should be shown to parents or the child (see Magistrates' Court [Children and Young Persons] Rules 1970).

In practice, different courts have different policies as to whether reports should be made available to parents and children, and as to how much of the contents should be revealed. Some courts may read the entire contents of a report aloud to a child and his parents, although rules only stipulate that 'contentious passages should be summarised by the court for the child'. Quite often this means that the magistrates will convey the gist of such passages in a language which will not raise the anxiety levels of children and parents. Seldom, if ever, are reports given to the child during the hearing, and probably never prior to it. Indeed, it is often the case that even a child's lawyer may not receive a copy of the report until he arrives in court to represent a child. Peter Jones, a London solicitor, expresses the concern of many lawyers when he says, 'It is impossible to provide the best standard of representation to a child, if you don't receive the reports until the day of the hearing. It concerns me that it is often difficult

*Despite this increased emphasis upon the need for SERs, there are still major differences in their availability. They are unlikely to be prepared for traffic offenders and the 'Borstal study' found significant geographical differences: the social services department in Wiltshire, for example, prepared proportionately half as many reports as their local authority colleagues in Bristol. (Priestley *et al* 1977).

to differentiate fact, opinion and interpretation in these reports which can make cross examination difficult. If you press a social worker in cross examination to clarify points of jargon you risk alienating the bench who may perceive your questions as being hostile to the social worker and the welfare ethos of the court. If you don't you are failing in your duty to the client to see that he gets justice.'

The increased status given to such reports is reflected by the emphasis placed on their correct completion in professional training courses for social workers and probation officers. It is not uncommon to hear graduates from such courses make distinctions between their colleagues on the basis of their relative skill in producing high quality SERs. The differences between the quality of the reports

---

Defendant's Access to Social Enquiry Reports

Number of times social workers informed defendants of right to refuse a report —

	YES	NO	DON'T KNOW
	11	62	4

Cases where defendant actually read or was informed of content of report.

Child	2
Parents	44
Both	14
Social Worker	
Gave precis or read it out	6
Not at all	20

(Anderson 1978)

(It should be emphasised that these figures are derived from totally separate statistics obtained by the author from two juvenile courts which were selected for their contrasting interpretations of their role in juvenile justice.)

The Language of the Social Enquiry Report

'A recommendation for supervision . . . may be phrased in a number of ways. Thus, what may be termed a "punitive magistrate" may . . . receive a recommendation for "an added control over his behaviour", while a welfare-oriented magistrate will be advised of "the need for additional support".'

'I talk in a certain way because I know how it will be received. With a social services magistrate, I'll talk of the needs of the boy, peer groups etc. — with a more punitive bench I'll talk about the seriousness of the offence and his attitude to it.' (Anderson, 1978.)

appears, for example, to be one way in which probation officers assert their superiority over social workers. Pat Carlen quotes a typical comment from one probation officer:

> The magistrate gets really annoyed when social workers are what he calls 'chummy'. They write reports and refer to 'little Johnny this' and 'little Johnny that' . . . not 'Smith this' and 'Smith that' and the magistrates can't stand it. I sometimes say to a social worker, 'When you do the report, do refer to the person by his surname otherwise the magistrate won't like it', but they can't get into the way. (Carlen, 1976)

Given such stylistic differences between social enquiry reports prepared by probation officers and social workers, what is the material which is common to most such reports?

It is unusual for there to be any regulation form on which they are written in that this is believed to lead to stereotyping but certain guidelines seem to be followed. They are divided into two sections. The first contains details of the offender, his personality and background, and the second, recommendations for action. The information which is likely to be included under these headings is perhaps best gauged from the suggested headings outlined in the Streatfield Report.* These include: offender's home surroundings and family background, his attitudes to his family and their response to him, his school and work record and spare time activities, his attitude to employment, his attitude to his present offence, his attitude and response to previous forms of treatment following any previous convictions, detailed histories about relevant physical and mental conditions, an assessment of personality and character. This, as Philip Bean points out, is something of a simplified list. A paper published by the National Association of Probation Officers lists eleven major categories and 91 sub-categories (Bean, 1976).

Now many of these suggest the need for an extensive and highly subtle analysis. (It is almost trite to point out that one's attitudes to immediate family, for example, and their attitudes to oneself, are, necessarily complex and ambivalent.) It is, however, unlikely that any SER will be able to do much justice to such subtleties. One investigation for example into the compilation of SERs (in this case by probation officers who are generally regarded by the courts as more adequate report writers than the average social worker) showed that an average of only 42 minutes was spent interviewing the defendant. Indeed, almost as much time appears to be spent on writing and thinking about these reports as in actually conducting the interviews upon which they depend.

Some indication of the range of familial questions which might need to be dealt with in this time is given in the insert on p.27. The reader might find that it is helpful to imagine answering these questions about his/her own family in a time period which when one allows for all the other information that has to be collected on such matters as details of the offence, health, intelligence, personality and employment — would average no more than 30 minutes.

One of the most conscientious researchers in this field provided a neat

*Report of the Interdepartmental Committee on the Business of Criminal Courts (1962).

example of how very superficial such reports can be as a result of this limited contact time. A social enquiry report relating to a particular juvenile offender had been read out in court and the social worker responsible for it had subsequently found herself sitting outside the courtroom with the mother of the child. 'What did you mean in your report when you said his father had no control over him', she demanded, 'You never even met his father'. 'Oh yes I did', said the social worker. 'He just sat in the chair by the fire saying nothing during the whole interview'. 'That', said the mother, 'wasn't his father. It was his eldest brother!'

Social Enquiry Reports: Questions on the Family

Talk about relationship within the family; whether there is any marital disharmony, and if it results in violence or rows or separation. Try to get an understanding of each person's attitudes towards the others, and their expectations of each other. What kind of discipline is imposed in the home, and by whom? What kind of moral standards are there? . . . Are the parents' ages compatible, or the children's ages? What do the plain facts reveal? Do they suggest separation of the parents from time to time, or what? . . . When you have a real understanding of his present family situation, ask him how this compares with the family situation in which he was brought up. How do the relative personalities and the demands they make on him compare? . . . Does he think his home is better than that of his parents', and if so, in what respects? . . . What of his childhood years? What sort of memories does he have of them? Did he have a good relationship with his father, or was the father overbearing, or authoritarian? What of his mother; was she a warm, outgoing personality, or cold and indifferent; an accepting or rejecting kind of person?

What of the interplay between his parents; was it a harmonious marriage or a tumultuous one? Did he feel that they were treated fairly, or that he was discriminated against? What expectations did his parents have of him and how far has he lived up to them? If he feels he has not done the things they expected of him to, does this trouble him? How does his outlook on life compare with theirs, and what has made the difference? . . . Does he see things as being better or worse? (Perry, 1975).

The readiness to indict family conditions in Social Enquiry Reports may take many forms; the following are taken from actual reports; 'broken home', 'impaired bonding', 'the mother's own mothering need', 'role confusion between parents', 'wife over-dependent on husband', 'mother relates to children more as a sibling than a mother', 'father plays a secondary role in the home', 'child's lack of affection from the family', 'breakdown of extended family and lack of kinship support'.

Much of this familial analysis is dependent upon a model of personality development loosely based upon psychoanalytic theory. Particular versions of Freudian theory, especially those promulgated by D.W. Winnicott (*The Child, the Family and the Outside World* Penguin 1966) John Bowlby and Mary

Salter-Ainsworth (*Child Care and the Growth of Love* Penguin 1965) D. Burling-ton and A. Freud (*Infants without Families* Allen and Unwin 1944) and in such recent publications as *Good Enough Parenting* (Central Council for Education and Training in Social Work 1978) influence not only the questions which social workers asks their 'clients' but also the way in which 'clients' replies are structured in the final report.

This is not the place to conduct an analysis of the particular validity of these theoretical accounts of childhood development. For social workers' use of such

It is perhaps invidious to select particular examples from social enquiry reports in order to illustrate some of the matters discussed in this chapter. Obviously context is important. But we found it impossible to exclude the following:

Miss B has been in her present accommodation since October and she is already in one week's arrears of rent . . . She kept frightening the children by telling them that going to a foster home meant going to live with strangers.' (Social enquiry report on an application to have a care order discharged by mother.)

'Add to this an unsatisfied longing for nicotine upon which she became very dependent before her admission to B House.' (Social enquiry report on 13 year old girl.)

'Mrs A achieves easy orgasm through mutual masturbation with Miss B, which they find mutually satisfying.' (Social enquiry report concering the mother of a four year old girl.)

'In C Lodge Arthur had regularly been involved in fights, has bullied younger children, broken windows and spit at the warden. During his visits to his mother's home he seems quiet and withdrawn. I believe that this indicates that Arthur feels more secure at C Lodge which provides him with a framework in which he can express himself more freely.' . . . 'Mrs D's own threshold of stress is low and she has constantly put pressure on Arthur concerning his return to her care. This pressure has caused Arthur great anxiety and he has constantly complained that he wishes to go home. If Arthur were to be returned to the care of his mother I think his emotional development would be set back.' (Report on an 11 year old boy in an application to discharge care order.)

'She told me that she wanted to go to a commune to get some carnal knowledge.' (Affidavit by social worker in a Wardship Case.)

'What I actually said was that I wanted to go to the commune to gain calm and knowledge.' (Affidavit in reply by the mother in question.)

models is fairly eclectic, and certainly many of the original authors would be heartily embarrassed by the transformations which their ideas have undergone in the movement from printed page to juvenile court.

This readiness on the part of the practitioners to pick and choose among sources is nicely illustrated by the comparative lack of interest which has been shown in this country in the 1973 book by Joseph Goldstein, Anna Freud and Albert Solnit, *Beyond the Best Interests of the Child*. For although this text subscribes to the psychoanalytic theory of child development (indeed, Anna Freud is probably its greatest living advocate), it also attempts to relate the theory to legal procedures and to social work practice by introducing the notion of 'the least detrimental available alternative' − that is to the idea that there is a requirement for social workers and others to demonstrate that the alternative to home which they propose is clearly more beneficial (or at least less damaging) than that which at present obtains. This concept is mainly raised in connection with adoption and the removal of children from foster parents but the authors also advocate its employment in juvenile delinquency proceedings. If adopted it would mean that courts would be placed under an obligation to be more conscientious than at present in contrasting the child's present position with any placement proposed by a social services department. This in turn would raise other issues concerning the availability of, and the nature of, evidence produced by the social worker. As Goldstein, Freud and Solnit observe, 'Many decisions are "in name only" for the best interests of the child who is being placed . . . they are fashioned primarily to meet the needs and wishes of competing adult claimants or to protect the general policies of a child care or other administrative agency'. The application of the 'least detrimental alternative' principle in a situation where there is firm evidence of the failure of residential treatment or penal establishments to modify delinquent behaviour would frequently make it difficult to send a child or young person to a community school, detention centre or borstal by the straightforward claim that it was in his best interests.

Another important difference between social enquiry reports, is the relative readiness of the writer to make positive recommendations to the court. As Philip Bean has shown, the predecessors of the Social Enquiry Reports − the reports prepared before the 1933 Children and Young Persons Act − were essentially evangelical in tone (Bean, 1976). Their aim he writes: 'was to protect offenders . . . from demon judges and demon drink.' The gradual official acknowledgement of the importance of these reports mainly meant that they slowly became an important element in the courts' decision making. They became 'recommendations' rather than 'opinions'. This is despite the advice given in the Streatfield Report, 'The probation officer should never give his opinion in a form which suggests that it relates to all the considerations in the court's mind. It is not a recommendation but an informed opinion preferred for the assistance of the court on one aspect of the question before it.'

Such a cautious approach is now not likely to be observed in adult courts and is rarely found in the average social enquiry report presented in the juvenile court. Of course, the more 'rehabilitative' ideals of that court and therefore its disinclination to regard its decisions as 'sentences' encourages the report writers to take a more interventionist stance. Reports are expected to contain firm recommendations and there is evidence that magistrates feel dissatisfied if they are merely presented as a statement of opinion for the general information of the court. A recent study suggests that the availability of social information did not influence sentencing so much as the availability of this information supported by a recommendation (Thorpe, 1979).

This close identification of the report writer with 'sentencing' or 'decision-making' means that it is very easy for them to enter into a collusive relationship with the magistrate to the exclusion of the client. Magistrates, for example are technically not supposed to read the report until they have come to a decision about the guilt of the defendant and yet Pat Carlen, who has conducted a systematic analysis of the operation of magistrates courts, is able to say that 'of the thirty probation officers directly connected with the Metropolitan Court, only three claimed that they would *never* discuss a social report with a magistrate prior to a court hearing' (p.77). Several were ready to justify such behaviour.

> I may put the information one way — for the client's benefit and then I might want to go along with my report and see the magistrate and say, 'Look, I *said* this — what I'm getting at is a bit more.' Uh — I'm not terribly happy about that because it does mean you're giving information that you haven't made public to the client — so it would be more a question of interpretation than of telling him anything that I hadn't put in the report. Like you know, if I put 'This guy's inadequate', or 'of low intelligence', I might want to go to the magistrate and say, 'Look, he's as thick as two short planks' (Carlen 1976).

The possibility of such discussions between social workers and magistrates, of the development of special forms of understanding which exclude the subject under consideration is actually given a positive sanction in the 1969 Act. One of the recommendations contained in the Expenditure Committee's report on the operation of the Act reads as follows:

> We recommend that liaison committees representing magistrates, teachers, social workers and probation officers should be set up in every local authority in respect of children and young people to discuss not only the progress of individual children in care or under supervision, but also more general matters such as the developments of intermediate treatment. This committee should be able to require police officers to attend where appropriate (*Expenditure Committee*, 1975, p.xvii).

There is no doubt that such liaison committees have become a standard feature of the juvenile justice scheme. Although no figures are available, it is likely that most areas now have meetings of such a kind about once a month. (Certainly in London, where each borough has a juvenile court — each court holds one meeting a month. In addition there is a quarterly meeting of a higher level committee known as the Inner London Juvenile Courts Consultative Committee.)

We spoke to someone who had been centrally involved in promoting the establishment of such liaison committees throughout the country and he explained that the initial opposition to such meetings has now been largely overcome. The objections had mainly come from the clerks to the magistrates' courts who had felt that such meetings might interfere with natural justice, in that they involved collaboration between magistrates and those who were party to the case. He described this attitude as 'traditional and hidebound'.

But it is certainly difficult to see how the magistrates might maintain their judicial impartiality if they are regularly meeting and discussing individuals who although perhaps already in care or under supervision, are likely at any time to appear before them charged with new offences.

This does not mean that the magistrates always see themselves as agreeing with recommendations and by social workers. One of the most publicised debates within the juvenile justice system in recent years, has concerned the magistrates' demand to have more say over the actual disposition of those children they have placed on care orders. In some cases this has concentrated upon the magistrates' claim that in certain cases they should be allowed to specify that the child be institutionalised in some form of community home, a concern which has apparently been promoted by evidence of the number of children on care orders who are sent home by local authority social workers. In other cases a more specific version of this claim is advanced, namely that the courts in certain circumstances, should be able to order not just institutionalisation, but institutionalisation within a secure unit.

This latter demand is frequently raised in connection with the allegedly more disruptive characteristics of the children who are now appearing in court, and the apparent frequency with which those who have been sent to open community homes, abscond, and then re-appear in court on further charges.

Representations from the Magistrates' Association were strong enough in both these respects to lead the 1975 Expenditure Committee Report to recommend (i) that when a care order is made agreement should be reached in court between the magistrates and social workers concerned on what should be done with the child and (ii) that when a juvenile already the subject of a care order appears before a court charged with an offence the court shall have the power to make, if it thinks fit, a 'secure care order' requiring the local authority to place the juvenile in secure accommodation for a period not less than specified in the order.

Recent research evidence does not provide much support for the assumptions upon which these recommendations rest. Social workers contrary to the impression that they sometimes try to create are not found to be a bunch of free-wheeling libertarians who casually flout magistrates' implied intentions by telling their charges to run off home. For example, a study by Michael Zander (1975) indicates that while 101 out of 224 young offenders given care orders were sent home, in only 39 cases was this because assessment centres and social workers thought that was the best thing for them: 62 went home because there was nowhere else for them to go. Similarly, Pat Cawson found in her study of 497 young people committed to care that half the home placements were due to lack of an immediate vacancy and in only 18% of the first home placements was the child sent home because this was felt to be the best thing for him or her. (Cawson, 1978) Neither does it seem to be true that the initial over-readiness to issue care orders can be blamed on an authoritarian magistracy. The Lancaster study of 132 young offenders found that this was far from true. In only 16% of the cases did magistrates make a care order contrary to the recommendations made in social enquiry reports by the social services department (Thorpe *et al* 1979).

So why should care orders be made so readily in cases often involving first-time court appearances and relatively minor offences? The authors suggest the 'simplest explanation is that there are frequently "problems" of various kinds in the child's background'. Problems can be explained and developed in the SER. 'In this sense, the fact that the child has committed an offence affords a convenient opportunity to take him into care: it represents an administrative device.'

The authors conclude: '. . . given that the amount of time spent in institutions is recognised as one of the best indicators of future delinquency; and given that, in some cases, at least, social work practice tends to increase, rather than decrease institutional experience, it follows that there is a very good sense in which social work intervention − or at any rate social work assessment − is actually helping to generate delinquency.' (Thorpe, *et al* 1979)

The assumptions underlying the magistrates' requests for the power to specify secure accommodation are no firmer than those which underly their anxiety about 'residential cases' being sent home by social workers. Elsewhere in this book we examine the dubious merits of 'secure units' (see section 3f) but here it is enough to observe that the magistrates' concern about the re-appearance before them of offenders who have absconded from residential care, derives not so much from any dramatic increase in the rate of absconding from such care (this has been very high for some time: a figure of 18% who absconded and did not return to their community home was suggested in one 1974 study) but rather from the increased possibility of magistrates coming face to face with offenders they had originally committed. For one effect of the 1969 Act was to place most community homes (previously called 'approved schools') under the local authority: a change which ensured that the offender was more likely than before to be committed to a community home in the area in which he was originally sentenced, and thereby more likely when he absconded and re-offended to appear before the same magistrate.

There might be less concern about the inadequacies of the social enquiry report as a cornerstone of juvenile justice if adequate opportunities existed in court for its assumptions and recommendations to be set against some alternative proposals. As it is, statements made by social workers and others about the child's home life, about his/her special needs or best interests, are rarely countered by any evidence showing that such needs and interests are even less likely to be met by institutional alternatives which are being proposed. The dubious status of some of the evidence contained within the social enquiry report, when coupled with evidence of social workers' predilection for institutional options would suggest the need for the following recommendation in care cases: *No child should be received into care or committee to the care of a local authority unless it has been previously determined that such a course of action constitutes the least restrictive, or least detrimental available alternative.*

Now although many of our concerns about the possibilities of unreasonable intervention in the lives of children refer to the dangers of unnecessary institutionalisation, we are not seeking in all this to extol the particular virtues of family life, to suggest that life in families is somehow inherently fairer or more just than in other institutions. Certainly there are anti-interventionists who make family autonomy and the right to privacy a cornerstone of their argument. The psychoanalyst Joseph Goldstein, for example, puts it like this:

> The liberty interest in family integrity and in the familial bond which under-lies a policy of minimum state intervention on parent-child relationships needs no greater justification for each of us as citizens in a democracy than that it comports with our fundamental commitment to individual freedom and human dignity. But these rights to parental autonomy and family privacy correspond as well with common sense as with our understanding as psycho-analysts of the critical need every child has for continued unbroken care within a community of concerned and intimately connected adults. (Goldstein, 1978)

But we would argue the case against the present level of intervention in a more negative fashion by suggesting that removal from home should only occur when there is clear evidence that such a course of action constitutes the least restric-tive, or the least detrimental available alternative. Home is not just the family, it is also friends round the corner, at school or at work, who help to place in perspective the possible unpleasantnesses, absurdities or even cruelties or family life. It is an area which is known, a set of familiar landmarks, a guarantee of identity. And against these 'favourable' elements of home life, we need to set the profoundly stigmatising experience of going into 'care'. Three excerpts from the National Children's Bureau project *Who Cares? Young People in Care Speak Out* (Page and Clark, 1977) (all written by children at present in care) show how the 'caring intentions of social workers and local authorities are subverted by the meaning given to 'care' by those who have had to endure it.

> Lots of kids seem to think that you're in care because you've been in trouble with the police and that, I remember at school, I was there for about two years and I never told anybody I was in care. But you see, something slipped up, and a few kids found out, and they came to me and said, 'What you done wrong?' Because, you know, they look upon it as a detention centre.

> When I first went to my school there was some money pinched and I felt so guilty because I knew I was from a children's home and I felt I was picked on, and I knew it wasn't me. But you can't tell anybody that. I was called into the office and I took up a riot. I nearly got expelled. I would have kept my temper down but what I didn't know was that there was a policeman in the other room, listening to what I was saying. And when they did find out who stole the money they didn't even apologise to me.

> What you want to get across is that you're not just someone's burden — you're there, alive. That's what it is — you want to be known.

2c. Representation of Children in Juvenile Courts

There would be less cause for concern about the possibilities of children being unjustly 'committed' to care, or about the assumption of parental rights by local authorities, if there was clear evidence of adequate opportunities for parents and for children to be legally represented in such cases. But unfortunately the 'legal presence' within the juvenile justice system is considerably less substantial than within comparable adult proceedings. Neither is the current state of children's law exactly an encouragement to lawyers to enter the field.

> The law as to children is complex, so much so that even the specialist lawyer is bewildered by its interspersions and ramifications. It is hardly an auspicious start to find that the definition of the word "child" varies with the statutes, so that a child is a child in one statute but not a child in another. Indeed, there is legislative hesitation as to whether a child is properly termed a child, a minor or an infant. Nor is the terminology only to be considered; there are also juveniles and young persons to be woven into the fabric. Apart from the interweaving of terminology, one has the grey areas where it is difficult to perceive whether one is dealing with civil or criminal law. (Jackson *et al* 1977)

In addition to the difficulty of unravelling the actual law, the lawyer representing a child is also confronted by the uneasy relationship between the principles of justice and welfare which pervade the law and legal proceedings concerned with children. A lawyer representing a child being tried for an offence is likely to find the proceedings in the juvenile court very much at variance with the principles which govern his work in representing an adult. In adult representation, for example, a lawyer is usually concerned to see that his client gets the lightest sentence possible for the particular offence. However in the case of a juvenile, a care order, which is perceived by children as being at the top end of the tariffs of disposal available to the court, that is the most restrictive alternative, is usually proposed as being made in the best interests of the child, that is, as the most liberal alternative. The ambiguous position of the lawyer in such a situation is well illustrated by a magistrate who told a researcher; 'The lawyer's position in court is very difficult. Frankly, I find them on the whole a bit of a nuisance. I find they don't really understand what the juvenile court is all about. They haven't really any training for juvenile court procedure. Often . . . they make impassioned pleas not to punish when it is the last thing we have in mind anyway . . .' (Anderson, 1978).

Several of the cases conducted by the MIND child advocacy service indicated that certain benches in juvenile courts so strongly subscribed to the welfare approach that they were often positively anxious to find a case proved in order that they could go on to 'help' the child involved. While in less metropolitan areas, the relationship between the local authority and the local bench was sometimes so close that the social workers and lawyers of the authority felt confident that their cases would be proved, 'no matter what the smart lawyers from London may try on'. In one recent case the 'child advocate' was informed by a lawyer instructing him that the legal department of the local authority accepted that they did not have evidence that a mother 'had so consistently failed without reasonable cause to discharge the obligations of a parent'. Nevertheless they felt that the court would overrule that mother's objection to the assumption of her parental rights, because 'we know our local bench'.

The essential conflict between the welfare and justice ethics is clearly illustrated in the case of R v K (1978) 1 All ER 180. In this case, counsel, representing a boy who had been convicted of burglary and made the subject of a care order by a juvenile court, was appealing against the decision not to allow the boy bail pending the hearing of his appeal against the care order. Critically, the case revolved around whether or not a care order should be construed as a custodial sentence. The boy's counsel argued that the boy had been taken unwillingly from his home and that as his future place of residence was at the discretion of the local authority, there had been a substantial restriction on his personal liberty. The judge ruled that a care order was not a custodial sentence in that the restrictions on the boy's liberty were 'no greater than those which may be imposed on any minor member of a well conducted family' and that section 12 of the Children Act 1948 places a duty on local authorities to give 'first consideration to safeguard and promote the welfare of the child throughout his childhood'. As one commentator acutely observed, 'I doubt whether the boy in this case saw his stay in an assessment centre in quite this light. In any event the 1969 Act specifically empowers a local authority to restrict the liberty of a child in its care which could lead the child being placed in secure accommodation. The courts would not, I hope, uphold a parent's right to exercise this form of control.' (Richard James, *Social Work Today* 1 May 1979)

A further problem is the fact that 'English law does not confer on the minor a general right to be represented in any court proceedings . . . Provision for representation has been unsystematically extended to specific kinds of proceedings, in some being mandatory, in others discretionary.' (Bevan and Parry, 1978) In wardship proceedings in the High Court, for example, the minor may be made a party and if he is, a guardian *ad litem* (usually the Official Solicitor) is then appointed, who may instruct counsel to appear. But there is no provision for ordering representation in proceedings under the Guardianship of Minors Act in the County Courts, or in matrimonial proceedings. In criminal and care proceedings under the 1969 Act the child is a party to the proceedings and therefore has the right to representation; the parent however, is *not* regarded as a party and is therefore not entitled to legal aid. This means that in some cases lawyers acting for children may in reality take their instructions from the parents, thereby making nonsense of the concept of separate representation for the child.

Of course the lawyer representing the child in care proceedings may be confronted with very real difficulties in taking instructions from his client. How does a lawyer take instructions from a six month old baby? How is he to evaluate whether the child's rights and needs are best spoken for by the local authorities or by the parent? Or indeed is it in any way possible to guarantee that the child will be represented on his own account if the parent is not also entitled as of right to be represented on his?

We would argue that apart from making both parents and children parties to proceedings in which there is a possibility of the child's removal from home, that there is a very strong case for parties, through their lawyers, to be able to call their own expert witnesses as to the needs of the child, the capacity of the parents *and* the capacity of the local authority. Such is the purpose of the scheme run by MIND for the past five years, a scheme which has consistently received more requests for independent social work and psychiatric reports than it has been able to provide.

The presence of expert witnesses speaking on behalf of the parent or child necessarily brings an adversarial quality to the proceedings. And it is precisely this feature which has appeared to some to be most threatening to the proper purpose of the court. Lord Widgery in Humberside County Council v D.P.R.

Representation

'Counsel are too judicial and have not had training in juvenile courts and very often don't have the answers that the bench wants. I cut the barrister out of the proceedings altogether and ask the boy, mother or the social worker, although formally I shouldn't be doing this.' (Mrs Pete Timlin, Chairman of the Camden Juvenile Court. Quoted by Melanie Philips in *The Guardian* 14 June 1978.)

(an infant) described care proceedings as 'essentially non-adversary', and declared that they ought to be an 'objective examination of the position of the child', and not a contest between the local authority and a parent. But an important legal corrective to this view has recently come from the High Court. In granting an appeal against a Crown Court decision to refuse to allow the fees of an independent social worker to be paid out of legal aid funds the taxing master expressed the clear view that care proceedings are adversarial.

Unfortunately the experience of MIND's Child Advocacy scheme suggests that even when a child is legally represented he cannot be sure at present that his lawyer is sufficiently knowledgeable of the law itself, or indeed that the lawyer who speaks for him in court is actually familiar with the circumstances of the case. Generally, in MIND's experience, solicitors delegate their cases in the juvenile court to either clerks or to 'legal executives'. Juvenile court work is complex, legally aided and seldom as profitable as other cases of legal activity.

The small number of barristers who are experienced in working in the juvenile court tend to be quite young and relatively junior members of the bar. In the London area it is quite well known that there are particular sets of chambers who perhaps through their identification with the civil rights lobby have tended to specialise in welfare and housing law. The effectiveness of this small group is sometimes amplified by the fact that local authority social workers and lawyers seem seldom to co-ordinate their activities in the preparation of cases. In many juvenile courts the local authority may be represented by a court officer who is a social worker and who may lack the advocacy skills of a lawyer. Thus even when a local authority has a strong case for the need for a child to be committed to care for his own protection, the case may be badly prepared and presented, with the concomitant risk that a parent's or child's lawyer will succeed in presenting a weak case more efficiently.

Arguments that the quality of legal representation should be improved in juvenile courts to bring them more on a par with adult proceedings are, of course, in direct contrast to the view held by proponents of the welfare view, that juvenile proceedings should ideally become *less like* normal court room practice. John Rae Price, for example, the Director of Social Services for Islington invites us to see the virtues of the Scottish Children's Panels. Such panels: '(a) meet in a setting which is not adversarial in which real communication with a child and his family can take place (b) and because cases are sifted by the Reporter according to his judgement of the child's needs, the number of previous police reports and the time that has elapsed since the child previously appeared before the panel, there is much less of a revolving door (c) the time available and the setting enable the panel to establish a much more individual contract with the child and his parents than is possible in England.' (John Rae Price *Community Care* 5 January 1977)

Recent research from Scotland does not however suggest that the panels provide the opportunity for any more real communication than that which occurs in courtroom settings. Despite the presence of lay members on the panel it appears that the 'problem' and its 'solution' is still defined predominantly in orthodox social work terms. Paul Brown's study of the hearing system in Fife indicated:

> That the social work agency has considerable power of definition of the situation; provision of information which the child and parents are not aware of (and are only told about at the discretion of the panel); and of recommendation. Much of this power was hidden from the parents and children and resulted in the recommendations being acted upon in twenty two of the twenty six cases where a clear recommendation was made . . . In none of the cases observed was any decision taken by a panel which involved putting pressure on any public agency or institution. In none of the cases observed was any recorded complaint made. (Brown and Bloomfield, 1979)

'Perhaps we have all conspired to create two systems of justice, one for the child and one for the adult, the former based on a treatment model which assumes we can help or treat the child, and that long periods in care do achieve this end . . . the lawyer must uphold the demands of natural justice, not be seduced by vague claims of welfare which cannot be tested, supported or verified.' (Leo Goodman — *Bulletin*, Legal Action Group December 1975.)

Other research cited by Brown confirms these doubts about 'real communication'. Sixty hearings were visited and in only two was there full participation by all the members present. The other fifty-eight had either been monopolised by the chairman or panel members. (Such findings have interesting affinities with those on communication in the juvenile court, described in a later section.)

This evidence of lack of participation by parents and children makes one sceptical when John Rae Price talks about treatment programmes which have been agreed on a contractual basis after an in-depth interview *(ibid)*. The contract is hardly between equal partners, and one wonders, given a more democratic setting, how many children would happily agree to a contract which would involve them being placed in a behaviour modification programme, or a private psychiatric hospital, or a community home in which corporal punishment is practised, or just being sent to a strange school in an equally strange part of the country for an indeterminate period of time?

2d. Out of Care and Out of Court

So far in our discussion of juvenile justice we have been talking as though the social enquiry report, the familial analysis it contains, and the social workers' and magistrates' formal commitment to the notion of the 'best interests of the child' were always paramount. This is far from being true. Many young offenders who appear before the magistrates will attract sentences which despite occasional superficial references to 'training' are recognisably punitive. In 1977, for example, a total of 5,161 junior detention centre orders were made. However, even in these the usual presence of a social enquiry report gave some credence to the idea of a treatment model of justice.

But there certain certain occasions in the juvenile court where the significance of the social enquiry report, the relevance of the family pathology model and the concomitant talk of treatment and rehabilitation completely disappear from sight. These are cases concerning traffic offences.

Such offences initially stand out compared to other derelictions because of a strong likelihood that they will lead to a prosecution and a courtroom appearance. Now this hardly seems explicable in terms of their seriousness. Few of them involve actual accidents and the vast majority are cases of having no 'L' plates, carrying an unauthorised passenger and having no insurance.

We even have some evidence that they are thought of as relatively unimportant by those most intimately concerned with juvenile justice. The 'Bristol and Wiltshire' study asked 66 'practitioners' (chairman of juvenile benches, juvenile bureau officers, senior policeman, social workers and probation officers) to rate a range of offences according to seriousness. Violence, vandalism and breaking-in were among the most serious, while traffic offences and shop-lifting emerged as the 'most trivial'. (Priestley *et al*, 1977)

This low-rating in terms of seriousness would seem to suggest that traffic offences were most appropriately dealt with by the use of a caution. After all the increasing use of the caution by police is in conformity with the 1969 Act's statutory recognition of it as an important alternative to court proceedings. Section 5 (2) declares 'A qualified informant shall not lay any information in respect of an offence if the alleged offender is a young person unless . . . it would not be adequate for the case to be dealt with by a parent, teacher or other person or by means of a caution from a constable.'

It would certainly be in line with the increased use of the caution by police since 1969. While the total number of cautions given to juveniles in 1968 was 33,703, by 1977 it had climbed to 112,289 (the slightly complex relationship between this figure and the total figure for juvenile offences is discussed in the separate section in this chapter on the caution). None of this increase has been accidental. The Police Federation has positively argued that the use of the caution should be even further extended (*Expenditure Committee* 1975, p.287) but the statistics suggest that traffic offences are very unlikely indeed to attract a caution. In the Bristol study, for example, 100% of the non-insurance cases were taken to court.

Neither does it seem to be the case that prosecution is favoured so much in this area because of the personal characteristics of the offender. There is in fact little chance of the police finding out about such matters, whether they be problems at home or school, problem of emotional adjustment or intellectual deficiency. For although the original intention of the 1969 Act was to make liaison and consultation between the police and local authority social services mandatory (Section 5) and although the Home Office Guide to the Act recommends such a procedure before action is taken, it seems that the serious decision to prosecute in the case of most traffic offenders is taken without any such preliminary procedure.

And when the defendants arrive in court it is highly unlikely that this lack of concern with their background, with them as individuals rather than offenders, will be remedied by means of a social enquiry report prepared by local authority social worker. There are no national statistics available, but our own experience of juvenile courts, and our interviews with relevant officials, suggest that the 'Bristol' figure of five reports for 114 offenders is a good indication of the national average.

Magistrates do not seem too inhibited by the absence of such reports. They find most of the defendants guilty and the vast majority of them (approximately 97%) are promptly fined (Priestley *et al*, 1977). Ideas of treatment or of individual justice are simply not raised, and what is more, the magistrates seem to use such cases as an opportunity to deliver lectures on personal responsibility.

There is no clause in the 1969 Act to suggest that such a large category of offenders (approximately one-sixth of the total of all juvenile offenders under 17) was to be completely exempted from its provisions. But then neither is there anything in subsequent commentaries on the operation of the Act — for example, the 1975 Report from the House of Commons Expenditure Committee — to suggest that this anomaly has aroused any interest.

Now in a way much of this argument may seem disingenuous. Of course, traffic offenders do not get cautions, or occasion consultations or elicit social enquiries, or receive treatment sentences. They are different from the rest. Acts like riding a motorbike without insurance somehow are not the same as other offences. They do not suggest some personality defect, the presence of an unsatisfactory home, some obvious family pathology. They are just examples of people who know the rules deciding to chance their luck and then being caught and getting their just deserts. Why pretend to be astonished at the different manner in which they are processed?

But how do we know that traffic offenders belong to such special category? Consultations and social enquiry reports have hardly ever been prepared on such people. As the Bristol researchers observe *'People who work in the system draw a sharp distinction between traffic offenders and other children, claiming that they are not usually in need of social enquiries . . . This belief is not based on any kind of evidence since it precedes and therefore precludes the very activity that would provide it'* (Priestley *et al*, 1977).

Might it not be rather more pertinent in the circumstances (and this is the reason for our initial disingenuousness) to ask not why traffic offenders are *excluded* from social enquiries and rehabilitation sentences, but why so many others are *included.* If riding without 'L' plates can be dealt with in such a brisk judicial manner, why not shoplifting, theft from parents, obstructing railway lines, burglary, criminal damage and occasioning actual bodily harm?

For, after all, we have not one jot of evidence to suggest that the sensitive individual approach to criminal offences committed by children is more effective than the blunt imposition of a standard punishment.

What we have here in the case of traffic offenders is, in other words, something which looks very much like the adult system of criminal justice. An offence is committed, the offender is brought to court and a penalty appropriate to the offence is applied, all without any reference to notions of the individual's familial background, their specific rehabilitative needs or their 'best interests'. The growing evidence of the peculiar confusions and ambiguities and departures from natural justice which arise when these matters *are* taken into account is beginning to suggest to many critics that we should seriously consider returning to a system in which all juveniles charged with criminal offences are dealt with in the manner at present reserved for traffic offenders. That is to say, there should be a strict separation between cases in which any intervention in a child's life is based upon a specific offence and those in which the primary reason for his/her appearance in court relates to intolerable conditions in his/her domestic life.

This does not mean that everything about our treatment of traffic offenders is satisfactory. As we have seen, they are at the moment likely to escape the possibly unfortunate consequences of being considered as candidates for a care order. But this 'benefit' is undermined by the decreased chances that they have, when compared with other offenders, of receiving a caution as an alternative to a court appearance.

The Use of the Caution

On the face of it the use of the caution would seem to be one obvious way in which large numbers of children who have engaged in relatively minor derelictions could be spared the necessity of a courtroom appearance with its concomitant risks of removal from home and the community. But before an increased use of this option is promoted we must examine the matter in a little more detail.

For, although there is evidence that the increased use of the caution by the police does do a great deal to reduce the number of young offenders before our courts, there are some grounds for believing that it may also add to the total number of young offenders who appear in the annual criminal statistics. That is to say, it may have an 'inflationary' as well as a 'diversionary effect'.

This is ingeniously argued in a Home Office Research Study by J.A. Ditchfield (1976) who points out that the caution may not just be an alternative to the court appearance but also to the 'no-further-action' decision or the 'on-the-spot' warning. Unlike 'cautions' such decisions do not appear in the criminal statistics and thereby serve to 'reduce' the official figure.

One principal intermediate treatment officer for a London borough said that juvenile bureaux were overpolicing certain areas — large council estates for example, or black areas. As a result, he claimed, there was a certain amount of hounding by the police, with juveniles being cautioned for extremely trivial offences. (From a report by Melanie Phillips. *The Guardian* 13 June 1978.)

Now the likelihood of a 'caution' being preferred to a 'no-further-action' decision, seems, ironically enough, to be increased by the presence of a police juvenile bureau in the area in which the offence was committed.*

This relationship holds even when allowances are made for the general upward trend in juvenile offences and for the greater likelihood of such bureaux being found in metropolitan areas.

We might regard this increased use of cautioning as unfortunate in its effects upon those individuals who might previously have received 'no-further-action' decision or an 'on-the-spot warning'. For cautions are used very much as evidence of 'previous offences' if the cautioned individual should ever appear before the juvenile court for some other reason. A Home Office circular urges that they should be so cited, even though the admission of guilt which is a necessary pre-condition for the administration of a caution seems somewhat uncertain — based as it is upon the threat of a court appearance if it is not forthcoming.

Such anxieties are far less profound, of course, when the caution is administered as an alternative to court proceedings. One particularly interesting piece of research on this topic by Michael J. Power (in Rosenheim, 1976) examines the use of the caution in those cases where the offender comes from difficult family circumstances — that is, the very cases which the 1969 Act regarded as most appropriately dealt with by the courts. Although he emphasises that the overall size of his sample (253) makes any firm conclusions suspect, there is a clear indication from the data that following a caution, such boys are more likely to keep out of trouble in the future than those from similar family circumstances who make a court appearance. 'Those most vulnerable because of their fragile environment do better if kept out of the courts . . . it may be that the children's and society's best interest are served by not further traumatising those already in a state of shock.'

Such indications of the value of the caution (particularly when used as an alternative to court rather than to 'no-further-action') are difficult to equate with the very great differences which exist between police forces in their readiness to make use of the procedure. In 1976, for example, police in Cleveland made half as much use of it as police in Devon and Cornwall, while Kent's rate

*These bureaux, which were introduced in many forces from 1968 onwards, are principally concerned with systematising the procedures by which information is gathered about the juvenile from such agencies as the social services, the education service and the offender's home. It has been suggested that their inception was in part a police step to pre-empt the possibility of social workers assuming 'decision to prosecute' duties as envisaged in some of the discussions leading up to the 1969 Act.

of cautioning was half as great as Wiltshire's.

As mentioned in our discussion of traffic offenders, the 1969 Act required close consultation between local authorities and anyone else empowered to bring an information with reference to a juvenile before the court. The consultations were to take place after the empowered or 'qualified' person had decided to lay an information, and had reason to believe 'that the alleged offender is a young person'. (Children and Young Persons Act 1968 part 1 Section 8). Actually, the qualified person need only serve notice of the decision to lay the information.

Another problem to be tackled in advocating an increased use of the caution (particularly for such groups as traffic offenders and those who would otherwise have been sent to court) is the actual location of the responsibility for the decision to act in such a manner. We noted earlier in a footnote that juvenile bureaux may well owe their inception to the police determination to retain right to prosecute duties and certainly there now seem to be very large differences between areas in terms of police readiness to 'consult' local authorities before deciding upon 'cautions' or 'prosecutions'. Such differences may often depend upon the past behaviour of the child under consideration.

The Essex police, for example, have developed a scheme for consultations with agencies such as Social Services Departments and Education Authorities in the event of a child being suspected of some criminal involvement. If the child has not come to the attention of the police before, the police are at first only in touch with the child's parents. Consultation takes place with other agencies only if the parents do not dispute the allegations, and if a caution is not given. Generally speaking, the consultations only take place after a second offence has occurred, and then only if the parents do not deny the allegations.

The authors have discovered evidence that in London the police have drawn up a 'blacklist' of children who have been in trouble before and who are known by the police. One juvenile bureau claims that the criteria for inclusion on the blacklist is that the child must have been to court at least once before and usually would have been cautioned before that. When someone on the blacklist comes to the attention of the police over a criminal matter, the child is taken immediately to the station and charged. The juvenile bureau of the police department, as well as the social services department concerned, are thus by-passed in reaching a decision to prosecute. The consultation only occurs when a name is added to the list. Then, the child's social worker is notified and the police are open to suggestions as to why a particular child's name should not be listed. In effect, it appears that the discretion over whether to prosecute, which was supposed to be a function of consultation between all parties involved, has been removed in cases where the offender has been previously involved with the police.*

*Perhaps this is just the beginning of a more sophisticated method for the police to keep an eye on those young people who raise their suspicions. A note in a recent issue of the *Law Guardian* suggested that the Home Office research unit was considering a study of 'computerised psychological policing'! A profile is built up on each young person beginning with their first contact with the police. A computer prediction of the likelihood of that person committing a crime is then used to determine police deployment.

In these circumstances there would seem to be good arguments for the limitation of discretion in the processing of juveniles, that is for the existence of formal criteria which would ensure that in specific circumstances the police had no alternative but to caution the juvenile or to record 'no-further-action'.

2e. Perceptions of the Juvenile Court

One of the most important requirements of natural justice is that those whose behaviour is the subject of adjudication should be fully acquainted with the nature of the proceedings which will determine their fate.

They should know the functions of those who take part in the discussion and the particular interests which they represent, and be aware of their own opportunities to speak and put their case, or to have others speak on their behalf. They should understand the basis upon which decisions are made and the connection between these decisions and that which initially occasioned the adjudication. All the evidence we have from young defendants and their parents suggests that the day to day operation of the juvenile court fails to satisfy these basic requirements.

Although there is some lip service paid to the idea of informality in the juvenile court ('Proceedings in the juvenile court are deliberately designed to be as informal as possible' — *Expenditure Committee Report* 1975, p.xvi) the setting retains most of the formal and dramatic aspects of adult justice. The bench is typically raised above the rest of the courtroom, children and parents are required to stand while being addressed by the court, ushers frequently issue commands to 'rise' or 'be seated' and magistrates place great emphasis upon the child's demeanour and posture.

There may easily be more than a dozen people in the body of the court who appear to have some function in the proceedings. These include magistrates, clerk of the court, usher, probation officer, social services department, court officer, local authority social worker, policemen and various witnesses. One of the most comprehensive studies of the operation of juvenile courts concluded 'In most of the courts we observed, little apparent effort was made to acquaint the children and their parents with the identities of all the officials present' (Priestley, Fears and Fuller, 1977). As one defendant put it, 'I don't really know who they all were in there. You don't take much notice. I just wanted to get out. The only people I saw were those two at the end.' (Anderson, 1978)

At least this defendant saw the 'two at the end' as the most significant ones. In another study half the children in the sample could not correctly identify the magistrates. Magistrates other than the chairman were described as 'helpers in case the judge couldn't read someone's writing' and more than half the children were unable to say who had actually made the final decision.

The failure of defendants to make positive identification of the magistrates is no doubt connected to the lack of communication between the two parties in the courtroom. Although it is regarded as a formal part of the proceedings that the 'defendant' has a chance to put his own case or to introduce some mitigating circumstances, there is little evidence that this occurs in practice. Indeed, in many courts, the juveniles say nothing at all. One study asked 'why' and got a variety of answers:

'I didn't speak in case I got something wrong.'
'You couldn't make them change their mind.'
'The magistrates knew what to do before I went in.'
'There were so many cases they were just taking them in line. There were too many cases . . . they couldn't taken an interest.' (Morris and Giller, 1978).

The relative lack of verbal involvement by children in court cases which at least formally are supposed to be concerned with them as individuals is most dramatically shown in a detailed study of the total number of communications made by the principal participants in the proceedings. Denise Fears used a shorthand writer to collect such data from twelve different courts. In terms of sentences spoken the following distribution was found:

	Number of Sentences	Percentage
Magistrates	5253	60
Clerk	1407	16
Child	690	8
Families	1377	16

(From Fears, 1977, p.137.)

The combined offering of parents and children amounted then to about 25% of the total, while magistrates and clerks accounted for 75%.

Of course, it might be argued that many children are too young and/or too inarticulate to do any sort of justice to their own case. But the figures given above do not suggest that their parents have much greater impact upon the proceedings. Their perceptions of the courtroom confirm this impression. In the study by Morris and Giller, only seven parents out of 29 interviewed felt that the magistrates were interested in them or their children, and many declared that the magistrates were actually against them. (Morris and Giller, 1978.)

'In their eyes, I'm guilty not my son. They gave that impression.'
If your child is on trial, you are on trial.'
'They sum you up while you sit there, including the way you dress, talk and behave.'

But perhaps the critical question we need to ask in this section is whether or not children and parents understood the reasons which led to the magistrates' eventual decision, and believed that decision to be fair and reasonable.

This is difficult to answer, of course, because we do not have any direct access to the magistrates' actual reasoning, but it is most damaging to the official picture of the court as an agency of individualised justice, to find evidence that a majority of children saw their offence and not their individual predicament as the most important factor influencing the decision, and only a small minority saw the court's role as a helping. (Morris and Giller, 1977).

Very similar views were reported by parents, some of whom, like their children, actually queried the relevance of social work reports to the proceedings. They objected, that is to say, to those elements in the proceedings which were not directly related to the offence and the degree of guilt.

The words 'conviction' and 'sentence' may not be used in relation to decisions made in the juvenile court, even where the child concerned is brought to court as a result of a criminal offence. This does not, however, prevent such a judicial model being uppermost in the minds of children and parents who participate in the proceedings. Thus, even a care order which is explicitly made 'in the best interests of the child' is most likely to be seen as punishment since it involves going away from home — it is 'understood as some kind of prison sentence of anything up to eight years'. Even an interim care order which commits a child to 28 days in the care of the local authority for psychiatric reports may be seen as a short prison sentence. (Anderson, 1978).

This view of the court as an agency which is primarily concerned like the adult court with matching punishment to offence necessarily engenders strong feeling of inequity within juveniles when comparable 'convictions' attract quite different 'sentences'. This seems to them, and often, to their parents, to constitute a breach of natural justice: it is unfair, it is inconsistent, it is hypocritical.

The final irony in all this, as Morris and Giller point out, is that the 'offence' and 'punishment' view of the juvenile court held by parents and children may be a far more accurate reflection of what actually occurs in court than many of the more formal accounts of the practices would have us believe. Certainly, research already suggests that juvenile court magistrates look mainly at details of the offence in decision-making, and that even the increased use of interim care orders represents not so much a new commitment to the rehabilitation centre, as a way of administering a brief punitive warning to the troublesome child.

3

Within the Institution

An American criminologist has referred to the American juvenile justice system as a 'four lane highway leading to a cow pasture'. This reference succinctly draws attention to the pointlessness of conducting elaborate and expensive enquiries to establish the distinctive personality characteristics and familial problems of individuals, without any complementary attention to the actual efficacy of the 'solutions' which are then imposed upon them.

In this second part of the book we therefore take the question 'In Whose Best Interests?' into the range of institutions in which disturbed, deprived and delinquent young people find themselves as a result of decisions by courts and other administrative bodies. Whereas the question of natural justice was to the fore in our earlier chapters, when we turn to institutional life, we find the issue of rights becoming more significant.

3a. Observation and Assessment

Early this year (1979) an argument developed in the columns of the social work journal *Community Care,* over the role of assessment centres. One writer defended the work they did in diagnosing and treating the children who were referred to them by the courts and praised the skills shown by psychologists and psychiatrists in determining which residential establishments were best suited to the individual's needs. He was countered by another reader who roundly declared: 'My experiences over the last ten years leave me convinced that the primary function of assessment centres is not to 'observe and assess' but rather to contain children.' Howard Smith, *Community Care,* April 1979.

The evidence, as we shall see, clearly favours the latter version of their functions; so much so that serious issues of natural justice appear to be at stake in the current operation of these institutions. For if assessment centres are not performing the task for which they were established, then the many thousands of children, who are at the moment detained within them on the courtroom understanding that such assessment would occur, have good grounds for being granted, if not early release, then at least an early removal to an institutions whose formal aims are less readily contradicted by its actual practices.

What then is the supposed job of the assessment centres? According to the Expenditure Committee Report on the 1969 Children and Young Persons Act, 'the assessment procedure is intended to provide a sophisticated analysis of a child's needs. For it to function adequately there must be sufficient skilled staff of all the necessary disciplines, an adequate number of assessment places and a suitable variety of possible placements for the children once assessed.' This is, of course, like any ideal description of an institution, something which is unlikely to be fully realised. But the actual operation of assessment centres in this country departs so radically from the stated ideal, as to be barely recognisable from the Expenditure Committee's description.

For a start, it is extremely difficult to maintain that the majority of children who actually arrive in assessment centres are there because they, more than others, require 'a sophisticated analysis' of their needs. Many children who are the subject of care orders made by magistrates are immediately placed in residential institutions such as community homes, without the benefit of an assessment centre's 'sophisticated analysis' (which would presumably determine if placements at home or in a residential establishment were indeed the most suitable to their needs) or are allowed home under supervision.

The 'assessment' that they receive in these cases is no more (or less) than a social worker's judgement. Now, of course, it could be the case that those who go to assessment centres display a set of psycho-social characteristics of especial complexity — and that therefore a rather more subtle analysis of their needs is required — an analysis which only an assessment centre could provide. But, in fact, the evidence is that many who go for such analysis are not so much distinguished by the complexity of their needs, as by the more expedient administrative problem which they pose, namely the fact that no other institution is prepared to take them. Thus, the assessment centre becomes primarily a place which 'holds' children who cannot easily be absorbed by the other facilities within the system.

The most dramatic evidence that this is the case comes from an examination of the amount of time that children spend in assessment centres. [Averages are not a good guide here because assessment centres are also used for children placed on 28 day 'interim' care orders and for up-to-28 day Place of Safety Orders.] For, although the administrators of the centres claim that the maximum amount of time needed to observe and assess is six to eight weeks stay culminating in a case conference and placement recommendation, recent figures show 50% of the children remain longer than two months and 13% are still in residence after six months. Nobody, it seems, wanted many of the children

---

I'm in a small home now, but I spent 21 months in an assessment centre, suspended in limbo almost, for no reason of my own. There was absolutely no privacy. To do homework you had to sit amongst 14 or 15 little nippers bombing about, you know, booting the table or coming up asking what you were doing, and there was just no privacy at all. You were not even allowed in your bedroom in the day. You were only allowed up there at set times to go for washes, etc., or go to bed. There was just no privacy. (From *Who Cares: Young People in Care Speak Out*, National Children's Bureau, 1977.)

in the first place, and the fact that they have now been the subject of 'sophisticated analysis', has done nothing to alter the picture. The assessment centre can do nothing to transform the characteristics which led to the child being initially placed in care and it is these characteristics which determine their acceptability to other institutions.

The principal of Cumberlow Lodge, a girl's assessment centre, recently outlined some of the current entrance requirements for a community home:

> 'The criteria for a girl getting into a community school are about the same as for admission to Roedean. She needs to have an IQ of 120 or above, be articulate, come from a nice middle class home and not be over 13. A little interesting neurosis is all right. She should not be promiscuous, or on drugs, or have a history of absconding. But if she has an IQ of 75, is educationally sub-normal, has BO and an unattractive appearance, she stands very little chance of being accepted. The greater her need the less likely she is to have it met.'

The idea that the principal function of assessment centres is to contain difficult and awkward children rather than provide specialised assessment services is given added weight by a recent report prepared for the DHSS enquiry on assessment centres by a group of Heads and Matrons of such establishments. This paper makes no reference whatsoever to the actual assessment tasks of the institutions they control, or indeed to the ways in which problems of placement might be resolved. Instead, it promotes the assessment centre as the ideal institution for containing 'persistent offenders and disrupters' — just the type of place which is needed by magistrates who are faced with the 'small, but hard core of children under 14' who cannot be sent to Detention Centres and Borstals, especially if those who are in charge are 'allowed to have corporal punishment . . . (for) the persistently disruptive child'.

A far cry from the institution whose primary task was 'the sophisticated analysis of a child's needs', but perhaps a good example of how to make a virtue out of a developing reality.

If indeed assessment centres are more and more becoming places in which to 'warehouse' difficult children, it may be unreasonable to complain about their failure to live up to the second requirement contained within the Expenditure Committee's report; 'sufficient skilled staff of all the necessary disciplines':

> The key to understanding assessment is that it concentrates on the kids' problems, not their strengths . . . Once someone is in assessment, everything the children do becomes part of their pathology. For example, a social worker's report says that Jennifer has moods, is untidy, and has trouble getting up in the morning. But then who doesn't? It this a sign of pathology? . . . Assessment is really just a long drawn-out process the results of which are based on what's available. There is the belief that somewhere there is the right place for each child, and it's only a matter of finding. Of course, this isn't the case at all. (From interview by authors with social worker, 22 February 1979.)

perhaps doubly unreasonable, in that we complain elsewhere in this book about the ways in which professionalisation may compound hypocrisies and further doctrines of non-accountability.

But at least for the record, and as a further illustration of the gap between the Committee's ideal and the reality, we should note the statement made by the Howard League in 1975 that there are assessment centres in the London region which are almost totally dependent upon staff obtained from agencies, and also the national figures, which show that only four or five per cent of all residential workers are professionally qualified.

Given then that by Expenditure Committee standards assessment centres contain inappropriate children supervised by under-qualified staff faced with inadequate placement opportunities – what might still be said of the actual assessment which does occur. Is it an enterprise which might in better conditions – for example, where placements were more readily effected – be a valuable contribution to our child care system? We doubt it.

Information on the actual assessment methods which are used in centres is difficult to come by. It presumably involves a collation of all previous knowledge of the individual children. But it is hard to see how this aspect of assessment could be conducted very systematically when there are such broad differences in the quantity and quality of such material. The Records Project carried out by the DHSS in 1975 examined the intake form used by twenty six local authorities representing both urban and rural areas – 'the twenty six forms had only four items in common: the client's surname, address, source of referral and date; but altogether there were 110 different items of information represented and a wide range of names given to the forms themselves . . . one Observation and Assessment Centre could easily find itself being supplied with information on a dozen different forms from a dozen different authorities. This makes any kind of comparison and monitoring virtually impossible.' (Tutt, 1977)

Observation and assessment made during the child's stay within the centre is not likely to have any greater validity or reliability. In recent years there have been increasing academic attacks both in this country and in the United States upon the absurdity of trying to measure a person's normal style of working, playing, relaxing and sleeping while he/she resides in an abnormal environment. And presumably not even the greatest defenders of assessment centres would wish to claim that their regimes had much in common with the child's everyday life at home. More 'objective' psychological tests which also form some part of the assessment procedures have actually become a civil rights issue in the United States with the claim that no child's future should be determined on the basis of a test of ability which fails to take into account his aptitude at performing complex non-academic tasks in the home, neighbourhood and community.

The hope that such internal (and external) problems of assessment might be corrected at the final case conference which occurs before placement, is confounded by evidence of the inadequacy of such meetings. In the 1976 study of Fairfield Lodge Assessment Centre it was shown that the information for such conferences was not only skimpy, but also displayed big gaps and actual discrepancies (Reinach et al 1976). But perhaps most worrying was the fact that little or no account was taken of the child's views on the matter. Even though case conferences are in principle deciding a child's future, (perhaps placement

'Success story' boy hanged himself

A 16 year old boy who hanged himself while on leave from a Manchester social services department assessment centre was regarded as a 'success story' by the staff, a coroner's court was told last week.

Tony Ashton hanged himself with his karate belt at his father's home in Holme on December 30 last year. He had been at Rose Hill assessment centre since August, *after nearly four years in care for truancy.*

The coroner, Donald Summerfield, heard that the boy had pleaded with his father to get him out of the centre. But in returning his verdict of suicide, Mr Summerfield completely exonerated the local authority. (*Community Care,* 15 February 1978). (our italics).

in a community home for a period of up to six years) the actual subject of the discussion is not present, and neither is he/she provided with anyone who might represent his/her objections or even draw attention to the 'discrepancies' in the evidence.

Of course, it could be said that the serious defects in this 'assessment' system are of no great importance at the moment, in that it is the availability of facilities which influences the final placement decision rather than the assessment profile. Durham Social Services Department, for example, have produced a study *Assessment Centres in Durham* which suggests that distribution to final placements appeared to be random even though distinct differences could be observed between the children who were so distributed. And research carried out by the Wessex Regional Planning Area suggested that allocation was made not on the basis of any sophisticated analysis but rather on such self-evident criteria as sex, age, offender-or-not, and geographical location.

But this argument can easily distract attention away from the central flaw in the whole assessment-placement edifice, namely there is not one jot of evidence to suggest that the various 'treatments' towards which 'assessment' ideally directs children can be distinguished one from another in terms of their efficacy. In such circumstances, to insist upon the further sophistication of assessment procedures, even to institute liberal out-patient assessment techniques which take account of the child's day to day life, is to compound a nonsense.

3b. Community Homes

One might feel a shade less concerned about the numbers of children who are sent to residential institutions on the sort of dubious basis described in Thorpe's research (see section 2b), if such institutions could be shown to provide some clear-cut benefits to those who receive their attention. We have already described the inadequacies of one such residential institution — the observation and assessment centre — and must now carefully consider the other main alternative — the community home.

In fact, it is not possible to review the actual regimes which exist within such establishments: there is not only a wide variety of institutions which fall under the general heading community home, but there is also considerable difference

49

between those which bear similar titles. The Dartington Hall research for example, looked at eighteen approved schools within one area and found significant differences between them in their methods and style of administration (Millham, Bullock and Cherrett 1975). Research by Norman Tutt showed enormous variations in the 'drop-out' rate of community homes in one region (from 15% to above 60%) even though the two extremes were both from community homes taking senior boys (Tutt, 1976).

As suggested by the occasional scandals which occur in the system, some are clearly run on authoritarian and disciplinarian lines, make frequent use of corporal punishment, and treat their charges more as inmates than as individuals who require special attention and services. Others maintain a more liberal and less punitive ethos and boast of the amiable relationships which exist between staff and children, and of the treatment facilities which are available. It should, however, be stressed that the establishment of such 'superior' community homes may depend directly upon the refusal by the head to accept anyone who it is felt 'will not benefit' from the facilities.

One common feature however, which must concern us in this text is the tendency for community homes to see themselves as chiefly concerned with delinquency, that is, to regard their charges as individuals who are in need of reform and change rather than simply as children who need to be provided with the range of material, social and educational opportunities which would normally be available to them if they were not institutionalised. This 'reforming' ethos persists despite the fact that, as we have seen, many of the offenders who are sent to such homes have committed offences which do not differ in any qualitative way from those committed by others not sent to homes. And despite the fact that a majority of the 40,000 children in community homes have committed no offence whatsoever but are present in them as a result of the belief that they would suffer from neglect or abuse if they remained in their own home.

Children in Community Homes (in thousands) (England and Wales)						
	1972	1973	1974	1975	1976	1977
Community Homes with observation and assessment facilities	4.2	4.8	4.8	5.3	5.0	5.0
Community homes with education on the premises	6.7	7.1	6.7	6.2	6.8	6.4
Others	18.9	19.3	21.4	23.1	23.4	22.3
TOTAL	29.8	31.1	33.0	34.6	35.2	33.7

It is the persistence of the 'delinquent' ethos in community homes which helps to justify a range of deprivations and restrictions which would rarely apply to the 140,000 or so children who attend the non-compulsory residential institutions we call boarding schools. The 'penal' character of the establishment is further compounded by the staff's obsession with the keeping of detailed

The Six-Monthly Review

'What is a review? I don't think I've ever had one.'

'They shouldn't keep going over the past. They know what is going to happen, they know what *is* happening and they keep asking the same questions about the past to see how much *you* know. Well reviews are supposed to help you for the future, right? You should live for the future . . . I want to know where I'm going to live next year.'

'What we need to get over is we ought to have a say in who is there discussing our lives. We ought to be able to speak for ourselves. And if we can't get our points across . . . we ought to have a spokesman for ourselves. Why don't the children have their own person they want to speak for them?' (*Who Cares? Young People in Care Speak Out.* National Children's Bureau 1977.)

records on the children in their charge, records of social history, family, school, behaviour problems, which may not be seen by the child but which may significantly influence the period of time for he/she is deprived of liberty.

> They just keep asking you all those questions about all the bad things you've done . . . at home . . . at school . . . thieving and that — they don't want to know about the good things.

There is ample evidence from studies of community homes that the staff's concern with delinquency, with maintaining petty restrictions, and with record-keeping, is complemented by the children's view of the institution as one to which they have been sent primarily as a punishment, for bad behaviour. A prison-like concern with what other people have 'done' in order to be sent to a community home becomes part of the subcultural chatter.

> See when this kid showed me around — I goes, 'What yer in for then', and all that lot . . . talking to him and all that lot . . . getting used to t'place . . . you know what I mean? Soon as I come in I goes, 'What you in for', he goes 'screwing'.

For those who have offended the punishment appears as particularly harsh. As Thorpe *et al* have pointed out, in many cases young offenders subject to section 7 (7) are likely to spend considerable periods of time in residential institutions whereas if similar offences had been committed by adults, imprisonment would have been highly unlikely (Thorpe *et al*, 1979). Successful appeals against the order by parents and children seem to be so few in number that they do not even feature as a category in the annual statistics detailing the circumstances in which children left care. The case conferences, which are held to determine the suitability of the individual for release, typically do not allow child or parent to make any representations and in most cases depend upon observations and assessment of behaviour in the abnormal circumstances of the community home. The objections which are usually raised to the power which indeterminate sentences give to non-judicial authorities seem particularly relevant in this context.

The subscription of community homes to the idea of reforming or treating delinquents seems to legitimate not just detailed day to day surveillance and control of most parts of the children's private lives — their friendship patterns, relationship with home, sexual interests, correspondence, allocation of spending money — but also their incorporation into a variety of experimental programmes.

A recent edition (June 1978) of the *Community Home Schools Gazette,* for example, includes a paper which reports on a Token Economy Management System (TEMS) which was introduced for the 15 youths in the 'intensive care' unit of a Birmingham Community Home. Under this system the boys were 'able to earn tokens by achieving personalised behavioural targets. Tokens are then exchangeable for a wide range of back-up reinforcers, such as extra home leave, sweets, toys, cigarettes, games, puzzles, modelling kits and so on.'

In addition, if any child breaks one of the basic rules of the unit, he is given a punishment card with a fixed penalty written on it. For example, the punishment card for smoking illicitly is 50 tokens (one wonders if it is possible to get such a punishment card for illicitly smoking the cigarettes which are distributed as 'back-up reinforcers' in the positive part of the scheme). The boy then has to earn 50 tokens before he can re-enter the main programme. 'Until those 50

> 'People think that if you're in care you must have done something wrong. The first question they ask is "What did you do?" It's not just teachers and other kids at school but it's kids and staff in children's homes. When you go to a new place before you've got your foot in the door they say "Hey, what are you in for?"' (*Who Cares? Young People in Care Speak Out.* National Children's Bureau 1977.)

tokens are earned he is unable to accumulate any further tokens to place into his bank nor can he consume any back-ups' (which presumably means, for example, that he cannot smoke any of the cigarettes he earned before the illicit smoking occurred).

We do not wish primarily to discuss the efficacy of this programme or any other similar programme — although our view of their possible long-term success must be influenced by the recent Home Office Research Study which eventually reached the rather devastating conclusion that:

Much of what passes for 'treatment' in institutions can also more properly be regarded as being concerned with reducing the ill-effects of residential living itself. For example, while there is little evidence about the long-term effectiveness of organising programmes according to offender/programme typologies, there is some reason to believe that this eases problems of control within the institution . . . when innovations in an institution are made, for whatever reason, they come to be regarded as guarantors of increased therapeutic effectiveness. (Cornish and Clarke, 1975)

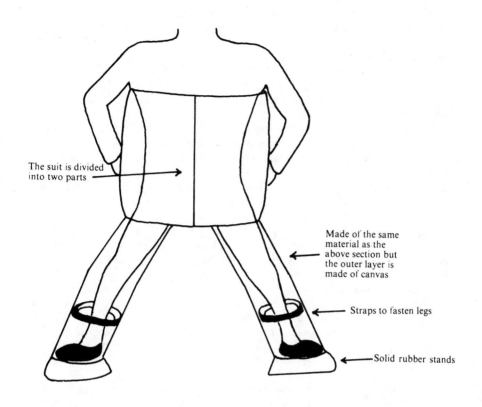

The suit is divided into two parts

Made of the same material as the above section but the outer layer is made of canvas

Straps to fasten legs

Solid rubber stands

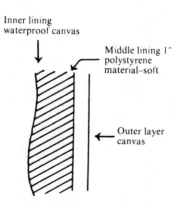

Inner lining waterproof canvas

Middle lining 1″ polystyrene material–soft

Outer layer canvas

What concerns us more, and perhaps particularly so when it is set against this overview of the likely success of any research programme, is the morality of forcing individuals to participate in any scheme which would not normally (or necessarily) form part of their experience in a non-residential setting. This particular scheme also seems especially dubious in that it transforms certain aspects of the regime which previously might have been regarded as rights or legitimate expectations (e.g. home leave, sweets, toys, cigarettes) into privileges which have to be earned.

We only know about the Birmingham scheme because its director decided to place his results on record: the possibility that we will hear of other such schemes — many of which might raise more serious ethical questions — is unlikely. The tacit acceptance that children in community homes are in need of treatment and may therefore be required to participate in whatever scheme is promoted, ensures that such matters receive little attention from either within or outside the community school system.

The extent to which experimentation may proceed without any problems of accountability to independent organisations is even more dramatically illustrated in another recent report in the *Community Home Schools Gazette* (July 1979). In an article entitled *Physical restraint as an alternative to punishment and maximum security confinement,* a Professor Lowenstein, who describes himself as Director of Lowenstein Therapuetic Communities, introduces his latest contribution to therapeutic progress: the padded suit. This suit which is illustrated below, has a soft lining inside and is stiff outside. 'It leaves the head free for breathing and eating and an iron stand is used so that there is no danger of the individual falling over . . . In only the extreme cases will it be necessary to use a gag.'

Professor Lowenstein defends himself from possible attack by declaring that the suit is not at the moment in use in the Lowenstein Therapeutic Communities and may well be less harmful than drug treatment or total incarceration. But nevertheless, the publication of the piece in such a journal can be taken in no other way than as an invitation to other psychologists in community schools, to make some use of it. Again, even though Lowenstein refers to (and eventually dismisses) the ethical questions raised by its employment, there is no hint that he feels the need for any independent examination of his suit or its alleged effects. One wonders for example, if everyone would accept that the suit 'is much like a cocoon wherein the individual is comfortable physically, albeit frustrated and possibly unhappy in being placed there against his will. *In a sense, it resembles the womb where there is safety and softness and yet at the same time a certain security.'* (our italics)

One is led to wonder, somewhat irreverently, what sort of case some predecessor of Professor Lowenstein's might have made for the ball and chain.

3c. Special Schools, Mental Hospitals and Behavioural Units

The role of 'assessment' in the recommendation of institutional provisions for children is not confined to those who appear before juvenile courts. Under the provisions of Section 34 of the Education Act 1944 local education authorities have duties to determine the children in their area who require special education.

The Act also gives the LEAs the power to compel a parent to submit his child for medical examinations for the purpose of ascertaining whether the child has special educational needs. If such a child is found to be in need of special education the local authority has the power to compel him to attend any special unit which they consider appropriate, unless the parents make suitable alternative arrangements. The School Health Regulations define ten categories of pupils who may have special educational needs: blind, partially sighted, deaf, partially deaf, delicate, educationally subnormal, epileptic, maladjusted, physically handicapped and those with speech defects.

In January 1977 in England and Wales 176,688 handicapped pupils or 1.8% of the school population were attending special schools or special classes designated as such by local education authorities, were placed by authorities in independent schools catering wholly or mainly for handicapped pupils, were boarded in homes, were receiving education otherwise than at school or were awaiting admission to special schools . . . *However, the scale on which children are ascertained as being in need of special education varies widely.* (*Special Educational Needs:* The Warnock Report, 1978, p.37 our italics)

The Warnock Report discusses the needs of widely disparate groups of children who are felt to have one thing in common — the need for special educational help. However there are many signs in the report that the exact number of such children depends not just on the intrinsic features of their condition but also on the likelihood of recommendations for categorisation being made, and on the criteria which are used in that categorisation. Some differences between areas are hardly explicable in terms of the objective characteristics of the population. For example, 'In one London borough in January 1977, ten times as many children were ascertained as maladjusted as in another' (*ibid.*, p.38.) And the most cursory inspection of the 'maladjusted' and 'ESN' categories in the table overleaf shows the dramatic changes which can occur over time. In 1970, for example, the total figure for 'maladjusted' was 6,093; by 1976 this had risen to 13,653. In the ESN categories the figure rose from 51,678 in 1970 to 64,711 in 1976.

Now it is not part of our present task to question the variety of factors which have produced such changes. It is enough to say there is a division between those who would regard such increases as a positive indication of the more sensitive and more widespread use of assessment techniques, and those who would feel concerned about social and personal implications of our increasing tendency to segregate difficult, backward, and disturbed children.

In some cases, of course, the segregation is far from absolute. While in the 'maladjusted' category approximately half the children are in boarding schools, a large majority of ESN children are in special day schools. But important questions of civil liberty are raised when such assessments lead to the actual removal of children from their home and their normal school.* For example, children categorised as 'maladjusted' can be compelled against their own wishes

_____

*ESN children are less likely that 'maladjusted' children to be placed in boarding schools.

Handicapped Pupils
Special schools, full-time pupils and teachers, 1950, 1955, 1960, 1965, 1970 and 1972 to 1976

		1950	1955	1960	1965	1970	At January 1972	1973	1974	1975	1976
Hospital Schools											
Schools											
Maintained		95	105	92	82	80	147	146	147	152	152
Non-maintained		15	15	13	10	9	8	9	8	7	7
Total		110	120	105	92	89	155	155	155	159	159
Full-time pupils											
Boys		3,604	3,477	2,692	2,271	2,012	5,106	5,689	5,523	5,635	5,537
Girls		2,972	2,999	2,159	1,694	1,493	3,520	3,986	3,930	4,037	3,929
Total		6,576	6,476	4,851	3,965	3,505	8,626	9,675	9,453	9,672	9,466
Teachers											
Full-time teachers		507	576	523	448	461	1,105	1,207	1,028	1,111	1,179
Full-time equivalent of part-time teachers		..	6	12	14	16	37	38	44	39	36
Other special schools											
Schools											
Maintained		393	514	598	678	788	1,242	1,277	1,315	1,337	1,353
Non-maintained		98	109	117	112	109	104	105	105	107	107
Day		299	321	382	454	536	949	977	1,019	1,019	1,033
Boarding		192	302	333	336	361	397	405	401	425	427
Total		491	623	715	790	897	1,346	1,382	1,420	1,444	1,460
Full-time pupils by category of major handicap											
Blind	Boys	610	656	718	681	601	566	588	587	644	679
	Girls	469	540	582	536	498	465	490	469	515	543
Partially sighted	Boys	853	1,081	1,103	1,115	1,248	1,319	1,302	1,304	1,331	1,338
	Girls	705	761	689	734	712	747	782	803	896	890
Deaf	Boys	1,844	2,218	1,932	1,721	1,841	1,893	1,927	1,985	2,098	2,084
	Girls	1,408	1,697	1,531	1,389	1,522	1,559	1,593	1,627	1,705	1,665
Partially hearing	Boys	566	700	812	933	1,120	1,178	1,249	1,285	1,340	1,261
	Girls	398	595	641	684	816	919	978	979	991	922

Physically handicapped Boys	3,258	3,410	4,073	4,330	5,035	5,716	5,811	6,090	6,995	7,290
Girls	3,128	2,903	2,976	3,155	3,795	4,115	4,224	4,399	5,229	5,468
Delicate Boys	5,706	6,678	5,948	4,864	3,908	3,403	3,312	3,121	2,904	2,883
Girls	5,047	5,589	4,672	3,602	2,542	2,151	2,008	1,891	1,817	1,706
Maladjusted Boys	467	1,029	1,426	2,305	4,793	6,966	8,172	8,857	10,140	10,232
Girls	120	206	316	599	1,300	1,986	2,322	2,726	3,387	3,421
Educationally sub-normal										
Medium Boys	9,205	13,633	19,640	25,571	31,388	45,894	46,946	32,068	31,727	32,599
Severe** Boys	..	..	..	..	..	..	..	15,480	11,290	11,857
Medium Girls	5,968	9,011	13,175	17,099	20,380	31,707	32,610	21,284	21,017	21,173
Severe** Girls	..	..	..	..	..	..	..	11,371	8,602	9,082
Epileptic Boys	433	475	416	464	581	744	811	860	1,294	1,358
Girls	312	320	327	350	434	515	566	646	911	973
Speech defect Boys	21	40	83	143	564	1,215	1,643	2,081	4,364	3,928
Girls	15	16	39	59	264	599	795	1,034	2,529	2,259
Autistic Boys	..	..	..	..	..	..	..	200	377	362
Girls	..	..	..	..	..	..	..	76	165	170
Total Boys	22,963	29,920	36,151	42,127	51,079	68,894	71,761	73,919	74,504	75,871
Girls	17,580	21,638	24,948	28,207	32,263	44,763	46,368	47,305	47,764	48,272
Total	40,543	51,558	61,099	70,334	83,342	113,657	118,129	121,224	122,268	124,143
Teachers*										
Full-time teachers	2,579	3,805	4,866	5,823	5,534	11,315	12,116	12,065	12,867	13,781
Full-time equivalent of part-time teachers	..	108	154	265	412	473	515	484	522	510

*The figures of teachers from 1974 relate to qualified teachers only and are therefore not comparable with figures for earlier years which include all teaching staff.

**These series reflect a change made in the method of recording the major handicape of pupils attending ESN (Severe) special schools: from 1975 a number of such children were recorded within a category of major handicap other than ESN (Severe).

Source: Statistics of Education (1976) Table 24 (29).

In late 1969, . . . Haringey Education Committee conceded that serious errors had been made; 47 per cent of the children in Haringey's ESN schools were black, and the percentage had been even higher in previous years (compared with the percentage of about 18 per cent for all immigrants in the borough).

Haringey Local Education Authority was taken to the Race Relations Board which, though it found no proof of unlawful discrimination, suggested 'a real need for a comprehensive enquiry into the extent of "overrepresentation" in the country as a whole and into related factors'. (*Mind Out* March/April 1979.)

and those of their parents to attend a special boarding school without any formal or independent hearing in which the child or the parent have the right to challenge the opinions of those responsible for the child's enforced confinement, or to present evidence on their own behalf to refute those opinions. A parent does have recourse to an appeal to the Secretary of State for Education who may review the case and overrule the local education authority, or a parent authority is failing to provide education suitable to the needs of the particular child, with a view to seeking a prerogative writ in the High Court to instruct the Secretary of State to order the local authority to carry out its statutory duties. However, as MIND has good reason to know, these procedures are cumbersome, slow and in the end unlikely to be successful.

The room for interpretation in some of these 'special educational' categories is most readily apparent in the case of the educationally subnormal (ESN). These are 'children of limited ability and children retarded by other conditions such as irregular attendance, ill health, lack of continuity in their education, or unsatisfactory school conditions. These children would be those who were retarded by more than 20% for their age and were so low graded as to be ineducable or to be detrimental to the education of other children. They would amount to approximately 10% of the school population.' (Warnock Report)

Children who are adjudged ESN according to such criteria and dispatched for institutional treatment have, as we have already suggested, rather less chance of objecting to the procedures which ensure their disposition than those who are the subject of courtroom care proceedings. What is more, those who are sent to special boarding schools may receive very similar treatment in very similar establishments to those children who are accommodated within the community school system. But there is possibly another common factor.

One of the authors has direct experience of running a hostel for young people from ESN boarding schools. The majority of boys who came to the hostel had no families to return to when they either left the care of local authorities or reached an age when local authorities ceased to pay for their accommodation. All of them suffered from the effects of a long stay in an institution and not surprisingly a large proportion gravitated to other forms of institutional care soon after they left the hostel i.e. prisons, borstals or psychiatric hospitals. They were in no way equipped with the basic social survival skills of obtaining and managing their own finances, cooking, budgeting etc. Most depressingly of all they seemed completely dependent on the hostel for any sense of their own identity. It is no exaggeration to describe them as having been socially crippled by well intentioned but ill considered care.

Interestingly, when the purpose of the hostel was changed from simply accommodating ESN boys to seeking to equip young people of both sexes with extensive institutional experience with social survival skills, there seemed to be no tangible differences between the new intake (who were admitted from psychiatric hospitals, community schools, prisons, remand centres, ESN schools, schools for the maladjusted and children's homes) and the old. The new intake was broadly just as intelligent, came from similar poverty stressed families and exhibited very similar personal problems. They were dependent on external controls for their behaviour, dependent on the project for a self image, dependent on the project to control their budgeting and hopelessly ill-equipped to survive as autonomous individuals in the community.

The Warnock Report deals with the needs of literally hundreds of thousands of children. In view of the fact that it proposes that complex, bureaucratic, and largely unaccountable, groups should have powers to, among other things, remove an unwilling child from an unwilling parent to a special boarding school, it is disturbing that the committee nowhere proposes new safeguards which might allow effective appeal to be made against such decisions by parents, children or their representatives. There is nothing in the history of psychological testing in this country, from Cyril Burt onwards, which would seem to justify an unqualified acceptance of the decisions made by its practitioners.

Admission of Children to Mental Hospitals

Some of the questions which we were beginning to raise in the last section, about the relative non-accountability of assessment procedures which can have serious consequences for the child, are also pertinent to the case of mental illness.

Of all admissions to mental hospitals each year 84% are informal, that is to say that only 16% are admitted under those provisions of sections of the Mental Health Act which ensure that the patient is compulsorily detained by the hospital authorities. But as Larry Gostin has argued (*Community Care* 5 November 1975) 'We cannot take the passivity commonly observed in many informal patients to be a meaningful acceptance of their admission; the unprotesting patient is not necessarily content with his confinement. For example, there is no genuinely voluntary admission if the patient fears that compulsory admission will ensue if he does not submit to the wishes of his relative, his doctor or his social worker . . . Similarly, if the patient remains in hospital because he does not realise that he is free to leave, or because he has nowhere else to go to, we should not feel comfortable in saying that he remains in care "voluntarily".'

Of the 10,000 or so children who are admitted to mental illness hospitals each year on the grounds of mental illness or mental handicap 98% are admitted informally. If a parent wishes to admit a child to a mental hospital, if the hospital agrees, the child can raise no legal objections to his admission; neither is there any way in which the child can seek to secure his release on his own account. It is well recognised now, in law and more generally, that the interests of a child are not always consistent with the interest of his parents, or the interests of the local authority in whose care he may be. A child whose behaviour is difficult and disruptive can cause enormous strain on a family.

In such circumstances there may be considerable pressure on a family to 'have him put away'. A child who is disruptive in a community home may be equally vulnerable to being placed in a mental hospital to solve the management problems of the home, rather than to provide his welfare as an individual. (We have been interested to note that private psychiatric hospitals are now advertising in the social work press.)

Mentally Handicapped Children

In the case of mentally handicapped children, many remain in large under-staffed and institutional hospitals in circumstances of gross neglect.

Maureen Oswin's book, *Children Living in Long Stay Hospitals* is a damning indictment of the official neglect of these children, and of the hypocrisy of social work's claim to be concerned with the protecting and best interests of children 'at risk'. (Oswin, 1978)

She describes how through lack of adequate care children become permanently deformed:

> The multiply handicapped children in Bay Hospital were pitiful examples of what does happen when children live for years in a hospital in which there is a permanent shortage of specialist staff. Some of the children had developed scissored legs to the degree that it was almost impossible to get a pair of pants on them. 15 year old Margaret, who had lived in Bay Hospital for 13 years, was fixed permanently into a sideways, twisted position, with her legs drawn up in a fetal position. It was impossible to place her in a chair: she had to lie on her side all the time, and because one side of her was permanently pressed downwards she could only see out of one eye. When she was fed, the food tended to trickle out of the corner of her mouth, as fast as it was put into the upper corner. (Oswin, 1978)

In discussing the part played by social workers in the care of handicapped children in long stay hospitals Oswin speaks of the failure of social workers to provide help in the community to the families of handicapped children and properly observes that:

> Social Workers seem not to recognise the deprivation suffered by children in long stay hospitals, and their failure to expect the same standards of child care in hospitals as they would expect for a child in residential care in the community serves to perpetuate the deprivation . . . (A Director of Social Services said that when he had been a child care officer and visited hospitals to see children who were in the care of his local authority social services department, he had thought the ward conditions were "very dreadful" but never said anything in case the staff were upset) (Oswin, 1978).

Children who are confined, often in circumstances of gross neglect, in isolated institutions and who also may lack the power of speech or the abilities to vote with their feet by absconding seem to have been largely ignored by society. That they are so ignored is probably because of the assumption that 'the welfare will look after them'.

Unfortunately, social workers' predilection for making sensitive interventions into the lives of children and their families does not seem to have been sufficiently extended to such institutional populations, even though, of course, the 'best interests' criterion might be most obviously contradicted by a child's daily existence in these settings. Instead they have been compelled for a variety of reasons to become identified with the more publicly manifested and politically sensitive issues of delinquency and parental neglect. Maureen Oswin's question seems particularly relevant to this one-sided conception of their role in relation to children:

I would ask you who is the most guilty of abuse or neglect? The father who batters his child in a fit of anger caused perhaps by mental illness, marital stress, drink or intolerable poverty? Or is it the society which then sits complacently by and lets that disabled child go and live for the rest of her life in an understaffed and underfinanced institution? (Maureen Oswin, quoted in *Community Care* 20 September, 1978.)

Behavioural Units

The increasing belief in the value of educational segregation, in the removal of awkward, backward and disturbed children from their normal schools, is not just apparent in the dramatic increase in the 'ESN' and 'maladjusted' diagnoses. Within the 'normal' educational system there has been the development of a segregation system which is not even based upon a formal assessment procedure, but which effectively establishes a special group of children who are placed in separate facilities on the vague grounds that 'they find it difficult to accept the normal framework of life and work in schools.' (*Behavioural Units*, 1978.)

The number of such units, which can be housed in such diverse accommodation as disused schools, old houses, and Horsa huts, has grown rapidly in the last few years. In 1977 there was a total of 239 units, 199 (83%) of which were established in the years 1973 to 1977. The number of places available by 1977 was 3,962.

The survey of the units conducted by Her Majesty's Inspectorate of Schools gives little guidance on the reasons why children may find themselves segregated in this manner. The initiative for admission could come from a variety of sources; headmasters, individual teachers, education welfare officers, social workers and probation officers. In some cases the units were simply 'sin-bins' for difficult pupils, but they also housed truants, children who had been in Community Homes, and children recommended for 'special education'.

The readiness to establish such units varied from authority to authority, with Liverpool and Leeds managing with two each, while East Sussex required six, and Berkshire seven. And if it was difficult to detect any clear and accountable procedures for admission, it was even more difficult to establish the means by which children returned to normal schooling. 'In general, teachers in units were more vague about the arrangements for return to normal schooling than they were about admission to the units.' The list of reasons given to the HMI team could hardly have been more eclectic:

> Some talked generally of improved behaviour and willingness to learn, while others were more definite and used criteria which included: completion of five consequtive days' satisfactory work and behaviour, growth of even-temperdness or diminution of adverse reactions; ability to assure the school that the pupil intends to work; conformity to rules; ability to relate to others; improvement in attitude and ability to hold his own academically.

The paragraph fatalistically concludes: 'The relative newness of most units meant that few had much experience of returning pupils to normal schooling.'

Now given that the quality of education which can be provided in such units is likely to be inferior in a number of ways to that which is available in a normal school — the buildings are likely to be inferior, there are hardly any facilities suitable for practical subjects — it is most disturbing that the procedures for referral and return to normal school are so vague. There is surely a strong case here for accountability, for the necessity of clear grounds being given for such allocation, and for an opportunity for parents and/or children or their representatives to challenge these grounds. Once again we see the growth of a segregation system which, while it may bring undoubted benefits to teachers in normal schools, provides no procedures for establishing that it operates 'in the best interests of the child'.

3d. Detention Centres

Nearly everyone these days, it seems, likes detention centres. Magistrates make increasing use of them: whereas in 1969 they sent 2,228 young offenders (between 14-17) to experience this primarily punitive regime, by 1977 this had risen to 5,757. The Conservative Party views them as a central part of their new law-and-order campaign, advocating the toughening of the regime, and more flexible sentences of one to two months instead of the present three to six months. Two new 'tough' centres have recently been announced by the Home Secretary. And offenders themselves, who make a realistic assessment of the various institutional alternatives in terms of the deprivation of liberty which each imposes, regard them as a preferred alternative to community homes, assessment centres or Borstals. Even social workers, who might be expected to look askance at such a crude punitive regime, find themselves recommending the centres, either in response to their own client's wishes, or in the belief that the relative brevity of such sentences makes them the least damaging of the residential alternatives. The prison department which is responsible for their administration does not issue an opinion: but their relative cheapness (approximately £104 average weekly cost) can hardly go unacknowledged. Altogether, never has the proposal in the 1969 Children and Young Persons Act that such centres be phased out for those under 17 years of age looked less likely to be implemented.

The Magistrates Association, somewhat surprisingly, shares some social workers' view that in certain cases the length of time spent in a detention centre should be cut down. Their suggestion is that in certain instances, such as cases of football hooliganism, courts should be allowed to sentence offenders for shorter periods than the present three-month minimum in the belief that an employers is more likely to wait for someone who is away for four weeks than two months. The sentencing practice to be adopted for unemployed offenders is not discussed.

Enthusiasm for the centres can hardly derive from any analysis of their success rates. The latest reconviction figures are for offenders discharged in 1974 and followed up for two years. The reconviction figure for those leaving junior detention centres (14 to 17 years of age) is 73% and for those leaving senior centres 58%: the overall rate is 64%. This failure rate is increasing. The comparable figures for boys discharged in 1973 are 70% (14-17), 50% (17-21) and 57% (overall).

The Conservative Party proposals for more flexible sentences and tougher regimes (in at least a few of the detention centres) seem unrelated to any evidence that such changes might affect their reconviction rates. The Home Secretary, William Whitelaw, was hardly illuminating when questioned on this matter by the journal *Community Care.*

Q. 'But surely "glass house" detention centres will have little effect on such hardened people and will be merely another step on the way to crime?'
A. 'Well, that is a matter of opinion. If you do not try how do you know? There are a great many people who prejudge and who say it would not work. But quite a lot of people who work in the system say it would.' (*Community Care,* 14 June 1978)

Whitelaw's attempt to rescue himself from attack by insisting upon the experimental nature of his tough proposals is hardly satisfactory. As Iain Crow has shown in a recent study, detention centres were themselves originally just such an experiment. (Crow, 1979)

Are too few young offenders being sent away from home?

The number of young offenders sent to penal institutions has risen rapidly since 1969.

Borstals		Detention Centres	
1969	1977	1969	1977
818	1,935	2,228	5,757

On the other hand supervision orders have decreased.

1969	1977
21,652	18,152

Perhaps Whitelaw, and his political colleagues are, understandably, less influenced by evidence of effectiveness, than by the evidence showing the popularity of such punitive measures among the general population. As in so many other areas of penal policy, results matter rather less than the impression that something firm and decisive is being done about the problem in hand.

The notion that young offenders should be subject to a regime of dubious effectiveness in order to satisfy popular demands for retribution can have little formal appeal to liberal critics of our system of juvenile justice. But at least those who are committed to a detention centre enjoy certain rights which are absent in the case of other institutional sentences. As a recent NACRO pamphlet commented: 'It is ironic that an unrepresented juvenile cannot be committed to a junior detention centre for what is now in practice a six week term, yet no representation or right of appeal is available in the case of a decision which may involve removal from home for a much longer period.' (*Sending Young Offenders Away*, NACRO November 1978.)

But we should not deceive ourselves that this punitive sentence in some way represents a clear-cut alternative to the more treatment oriented placements: recent evidence indicates that in some junior detention centres as many as 50% of the boys are subject to a care order. That is to say, they are children who have continued to offend while under supervision within the community or following their placement in a community school. Social workers who bring such offenders back before the courts may obscure the shift from care to punishment by suggesting that their client now requires 'a structured environment in which the firmest possible controls can be exercised' but the regular imposition of a detention centre sentence in response to such a request makes it abundantly clear that, in Norman Tutt's words 'Prison department establishments are becoming part of the repertoire of placement for children on a care order'. (*Social Work Today*, 4 April 1978.)

3e. Borstal

The 1961 Criminal Justice Act reduced the minimum age for Borstal training to 15 years. It also made it easier to transfer young people from Approved School to Borstal and reintegrated the Borstal institution into the mainstream of the prison system, thus making possible the progression of the trainee from the Borstal directly into the prison. In effect it created a continuum between the Approved School and the prison, thus undermining the role of the Borstal as an alternative to the prison system and turning it instead into a primary punitive institution which acted as a funnel to the prison system. This integration initiated the decline of the training component and the growth of the disciplinary and punitive aspects of the institution. Whereas Borstal staff had previously had a specific commitment to work with young offenders, in the new structure prison officers and assistant governors were allocated to Borstal institutions more or less randomly. Working in the Borstal is regarded by many of the staff as an obstacle to promotion since such work is generally held in low esteem within the prison service. New staff bring to the Borstal experience attitudes developed in the mainstream of the prison system and are seldom, if ever, offered the opportunity to explore alternative approaches which might be more suited to the needs of the Borstal population. The policy of regularly relocating those staff, who have some power to influence the nature of the regime in the governor grades, ensures that any experimental innovations are short-lived. This serves to justify the widely held view that only the tried and trusted regime of the adult prison system actually 'works'.

While the 1961 Act cleared the way for more punitive sanctions to be applied to young offenders, the Home Office argued that only a few young people under 17 would ever enter the Borstal but that it was necessary to have this sanction available for use in exceptional cases. The reality has been very different. The period 1965 to 1977 saw the steady decline of the Approved School and its post-1969 Children and Young Persons Act successor, the Community Home (with Education), and the rapid growth of the Borstal population from 4,234 in 1965 to 8,625 in 1977. More alarmingly the proportion of young people under the age of 17 rose from approximately one-eighth in 1965 to something under one-third of the total Borstal population in 1977.*Research by Millham *et al* (1978) indicates that the majority of these young people are less difficult and pose less of a threat than a parallel sample drawn from the old Senior Approved School. He also suggests that while the Borstal sample had committed slightly more offences than the other boys, these offences were no more serious and, indeed, in most cases were fairly trivial.

In short, in the 1960s the Borstal was redefined as a primarily punitive institution and came to act as an expansion tank for a declining and under-resourced child care system, with the consequence that younger and less difficult young people have increasingly been subject to tougher punishment. Partly as a consequence of these processes the reconviction rate which stayed at 30% throughout the 1930s rocketed in the 1960s and 1970s to 70% for the Borstal population as a whole and 79% for 15 and 16 year olds. The prison system has reacted to these depressing statistics by suggesting that the high failure rate is a consequence of 'the poor quality of receptions', but as Little has demonstrated even if this were the case the decline in the effectiveness of Borstal training also holds true for 'receptions of a similar quality' to those in the 1930s (Little, 1962).** What this suggests is that there is something about the Borstal experience which actually generates the criminality it was supposedly established to eradicate.

Rewards and Punishments

The outstanding features of the Borstal are the structure and organisation of the regime, both in terms of the punishment and reward system which operates and the way in which the length of the sentence is determined. As part of the prison system, the Borstal and its disciplinary procedures mirror in many ways those of the adult prison.

Trainees who have committed what are considered to be minor infringements against the Borstal rules can be subject to a Review Board which is operated by the assistant governor or a prison officer and can result in loss of 'association'

*484 out of 3,750 in 1965, 1,935 out of 6,690 in 1977.

**It seems clear that the current government's commitment to 'Law and Order' can only mean the expansion of punitive Borstal-type provision and severe cutbacks in Local Authority Social Services Department provision for young people in trouble. This suggests that a growing number of younger and less difficult young people will be subjected to the Borstal experience. If this is the case, we must anticipate that the failure rate will rise even higher.

(time spent with other trainees in leisure pursuits such as playing records), loss of money for the work that they have undertaken, or a reduced 'rating' which symbolises their behavioural and attitudinal performance and thus the privileges to which they are entitled. The next stage of what might be described as this internal tariff system is the Governor's Report, and more serious transgressions will result in the trainee appearing before a Board of Visitors, composed of the Governor, prison officers representing the section of the Borstal in which the boy is housed, and lay members (many of whom are in fact members of the prison and justice systems). Adjudication in these last two cases may result in loss of time — the extension of the Borstal sentence — or what is euphemistically called 'removal from house', that is, solitary confinement within a cell for up to 28 days. The boy will remain alone in his cell apart from a visit from the Borstal doctor and the Governor to determine whether he is surviving psychologically. Books and writing materials are the distractions for the day, apart from the arrival of meals and the mattress to sleep on which is delivered at night and taken away in the morning. The cell is bare, a wooden plinth being the only article of furniture. Being 'down the block', as solitary confinement in the cells is called by the trainees, is something with which many boys are familiar, and for a minority will be a common and recurrent event during their time in the Borstal. Their experience of the cells is well expressed by one trainee who said:

> First of all I was scared and then I got used to it. I stopped reading after a few days. I just slept all the time. When I had to leave I was frightened. I didn't want to go out.

Perhaps one of the most potent means of control is the use of the indeterminate length of the Borstal sentence. Trainees may be held from a minimum of six months to a maximum of two years. Boys are anxious to get their dates, but possession of them is not final or certain, their removal being one way to control their behaviour.

The control and containment of behaviour can, of course, also be affected by the handing out of rewards — gaining privileges vis à vis other trainees, being chosen for the 'good' work parties, and being given the opportunity to do community service outside of the Borstal. Although participating in some kind of community service can, and often is, a rewarding experience for these boys it is also a means of controlling them and because of this can mar and contaminate the nature and purpose of this experience. We might ask, if these boys can sustain the kind of relationships demanded by community service, why is it considered necessary to place them in the security of the Borstal in the first place. Many of the boys are able to articulate very clearly what they get out of doing work of this kind:

> It took me some time to get used to being on the staff, after this place. At first I would think that the other staff meant me when they told people to do things. The people were mental you know, handicapped, and at first I thought they were weird but by the end of it I liked some of them a lot. It's not their fault they're mental. You have to be careful not to get to like them too much and not to let them depend on you because you are only

there for a short time. It wouldn't be fair, it wouldn't help them.

It should be noted that the control of behaviour by reward and punishment may be supplemented by the use of medication. Drugs which quieten and contain the behaviour of those trainees whom the staff define as violent and aggressive are sometimes used:

> I cut my wrist because I was fed up with it. When they came in and saw me they dragged me out. One of them had me round the neck nearly strangling me. I said 'I can walk you bastard'. He squeezed me tighter and I bit his thumb. Down in the hospital they gave me an injection because he said I was getting violent. I was out for fourteen hours. When I came out of the hospital I was charged with assault.

While the trainees understand this system of rewards and punishments their understanding of the criteria by which these sanctions are invoked remains vague. A rule book exists and many of them see it briefly when they are admitted, but their ability to grasp the rules is obviously limited by the tension and emotional circumstances which surround being admitted to Borstal. In fact, they have to learn the rules of the game as they go along, often only finding out in retrospect that they have broken a rule. From the boys' own accounts, what appears dominant is a marked lack of consistency in the relationship between offences within the Borstal and the internal tariff system which operates to control these. As time goes on the trainees become aware that the same type of offence may be responded to differently depending on who is committing the act, and the prison officer operating the tariff system. The rule book is often cited and seldom viewed and ignorance of its specific content extends to the staff who work on the assumption that most things are not allowed. This serves to mystify power and control even further.

Surviving on the Wing

Simply to describe the reward and punishment procedures of the Borstal does not give us any clear understanding of how those within the regime adapt and and respond to it. We have to understand that control of behaviour is seen by the 'organisation' as part of the process of helping, caring for, and rehabilitating the young offender. The spectre of care and control reappears here as well.

How do the boys understand this? Many will respond to this confusion of care and control by stating a preference to be left along to 'do bird' in much the same way as an adult prisoner, rather than to succumb to what they see as the illusion of help offered by some members of the prison service. One trainee had this to say:

> What does this place do to you, it's supposed to help you isn't it, but if you go to one of the screws with a problem it's all round the place and then later someone comes back and says — yes, you are the bloke who's worried about your mum's divorce — like that, in front of everybody. I learnt fucking quick. If you've got a problem, bottle it. What they don't know they can't use against you.

When the offer of help and support is provided inconsistently, as it often is, and may be withdrawn and replaced by the operation of the punishment system, this is coherently expressed by the boys as being 'stitched up'. In other words they feel manipulated and abused.

Their response to the confusion between care and control, and the inconsistency of the control system itself, can take a number of forms. Some may defend themselves against the incursions of the system and its frustrations by violence against the staff or the trainees. They may stop co-operating with, or accepting the logic of, the reward and punishment system at every point, knowing that the Borstal has the power to contain them for no longer than two years. You can only lose so much time, so many privileges, do the most degrading work, but what it also means is that solitary confinement within the 'block' may be a regular experience. Indeed, for some boys 'removal from house' is a way of gaining some space and privacy in a regime which provides little of this. One boy explained his actions in this way:

> I don't want to go out, they won't make me. They say you've got to leave but they can't make me sign my discharge. I've got them now, they keep putting me down the block and I say 'good'. I like it. That really gets them going, there's nothing they can do about it.

For these boys, neither the 'carrot nor the stick' can control their behaviour or attitudes. They attack, but in a defensively violent way, a regime which they see as having little relevance to the way their life has been or is likely to be in the future. This is not a romantic notion as we have shown that the Borstal provides no evidence for either training or rehabilitating them, or helping them to solve difficult areas of their life whose source is located outside of the Borstal. Paradoxically, however, this accommodation to Borstal life, however defensive, prepares many of them to accept fatalistically the possibility of doing more 'bird' within the juvenile and possibly the adult prison system, and indeed, provides them with a repertoire of behaviour which only allows them to survive in institutions of this kind. This is particularly true of young people who have few sources of support beyond the Borstal.

The staff response to this particular kind of trainee is often one of matching a sanction with every transgression, but in the knowledge that ultimately neither side 'wins'. For these, the most vulnerable trainees, it is a question of containment until the point of maximum sentence, but in recognition of the fact that the boys are likely to return to Borstal in the not too distant future. There is a fatalistic acceptance that the system has no way of dealing with such a response and it reinforces the notion that the Borstal is about containment not rehabilitation or caring. A scene at dinner time where the boys were asked to eat in silence so that orders and announcements can be communicated, highlights this form of staff reaction:

> The Officer speaks: 'Right you lot, as far as I'm concerned you are all shit, and so you get treated like shit. Most of you will be back here and when I see you coming through the door, do you know what I'll do, I'll laugh my fucking head off.' End of address.

Despite this, however, the ethos of discipline and a belief in its ability to affect the young offender's behaviour is doggedly held on to by the officers. For some officers this provides a perplexing and difficult dilemma, for others it is accepted as just part of the job, the rationale and purpose of their job unexplored by them other than at a very crude level. Some say that they are not paid enough to spend time worrying about what they are doing, let alone the welfare of the boys.

Another form of accommodation to the Borstal is for the boys to 'play the game' by using the reward system to make life as easy and as less intrusive as possible. Whilst they may be the line of least resistance to achieve a quiet life, it also means passively accepting what may be the harsh and inconsistent responses of some prison officers – being pushed around and sometimes physically and verbally abused by prison officers, and perhaps other trainees. Bullying and coercion are accepted in the knowledge that 'grassing', or trying to obtain some justice in the face of injustice, will result in further abuse and aggression. Such an incident was described thus:

We were pissing about after lights out. He wasn't doing as much as us – just laughing. These two screws had him cause he always makes a noise. So they came over and said 'OK you're nicked'. He says, 'I never done it'. They called him a lying bastard and one punched him and the other one kicked him in the back. I said 'leave it out you bastards – he's only 15' and they said 'shut up or you will get nicked too.' They took him down the block and gave him a right kicking. Look at the boot mark on his face. I said I'd go to the 'governors' as a witness but – (a prison officer) said that if I did he'd stitch me up and I'd do the full two years, so I swallowed it.

Injustice in this situation cannot be rectified as problems are individualised and divisions within the inmate population are used as a form of control. For these boys, a Borstal 'failure' is thought to be a trainee who stays longer than a year – someone who has made trouble for himself rather than accepting and using the logic of the reward and punishment system. It is interesting that this definition of the 'borstal failure' used by the boys mirrors the statistic that the average borstal sentence is nine to eleven months. Confirmation, that their views of the regime reflects that of the formal system.

Lastly, there are some boys who react to the regime, not by acting against it or using it in some kind of systematic way, but by turning their anxiety and anger in on themselves. They abuse and damage themselves physically, perhaps by cutting their wrists, slashing other parts of their bodies, or by burning themselves. Sometimes this will result in their being removed to hospital or other parts of the Borstal, perhaps a welcome but transitory respite from the physical and emotional intrusions of the regime. In some instances this may be responded to in a humane and caring way by prison staff, but in others out of fear that if something were to go seriously wrong – if a boy were to die – disciplinary action would be visited upon themselves.

To some extent the kind of response adopted by the boys will be reflected in the length of time served, but again the inconsistent responses by prison staff do not make this relationship a necessary or particularly strong one. What does appear to be the case is that for the majority, the Borstal system is processing them fairly quickly — many not staying for more than a year — but for an

---

From Institution to Institution

One recent survey indicated that 42% of *junior detention centre* inmates had previous institutional experience.

Over 33% had spent some time in a community home.

Over half the *Borstal* trainees surveyed had previously been to a junior detention centre.

Nearly one half had spent some time in an approved school or children's home. (From *Fifteen and Sixteen Year Olds in Borstal,* Young Offenders Psychology Unit, Home Office, 1977.)

---

identifiable minority periods in excess of eighteen months are possible. More often than not these will be those boys who have refused to accept or use the system, but react to it in what we have called a defensively violent way.

Whatever response the trainee adopts to the regime it is an attempt to hold onto his own identity — some manage it, some don't. What he is trying to do is gain some control in a situation of powerlessness. Some of the prison officers try to 'penetrate' and understand the meaning of the boy's behaviour, but in many fundamental ways it is not in their interest to dig beneath the surface since it is the fundamental values of the Borstal which are being challenged.

On the Out — A Temporary Phenomenon

It is often the case that the better they have learned to survive in the institution, the greater will be their fear and anxiety about getting out. This is graphically called 'gate fever'. Boys may deliberately engage in acts which invoke sanctions that prolong their stay, delay their home visit (a preparation for leaving), or curtail the likelihood of doing community service. Boys who have finally been given their target dates, which have previously been so jealously guarded, engage in discussion which suggests that 'they quite like it in here, and anyway what is there for you on the outside'. Near to the day of release arguments may ensue between the boys about whether the trainee in question will 'be back' and if so how long it will take.

Ways of surviving and preparing for the 'outside' are not dominant themes, either for the boys or, it seems, for the prison staff. The daily work that they undertake in the Borstal hardly equips them with new skills or a practical interest which they can use in employment once they are released. Indeed, for many unemployment looms large. Contact with probation officers or social workers during and after the Borstal sentence is not seen by the boys as being of much help. However overburdened these workers are, to the boys it just seems that they were the ones, by their recommendations at court, who put them in the Borstal and now they are forgotten. Feelings of separation from the life outside of the Borstal, and in many cases a lack of any support network which they can effectively use when released, means that the Borstal trainees will often seek each other's company when outside knowing that at least they share similar experiences, both past and present. Indeed, some boys go back voluntarily because they find themselves unable to cope with an unregimented life. A regime which they have tried to reject, in whatever way, may when on the outside come to assume different proportions — as somewhere where you know that there is a bed for you, food, and the daily grind of work.

Borstal and the Law and Order Game

In conventional terms Borstal 'worked' in the 1930s: it responded to the problems of the time in a way which was understandable at that time. Borstal in the 1960s and 1970s is little short of a disaster, systematically generating the very problems which it is supposed to be solving. It seems fairly clear that the integration of the Borstal into the mainstream of the prison system in the 1960s has resulted in its absorbing all the problems to which that system is heir. In particular it has taken on the very high reconviction rates which characterises the adult prison system, while the population has simultaneously become larger, younger and by almost all criteria, less problematic.

Attempts at reform and innovation in the post-war period have been sporadic and short lived due to the crippling administrative and procedural obstacles which ensure that the system will always eventually revert to the regime of a traditional prison.

A recent report by NACRO (1977) has estimated that no more than 400 young people need be kept in secure conditions and yet the Borstals are bulging at the seams. This situation is brought about in part by the economic imperatives which guide cuts in local authority social services expenditure, and the consequent inability of the social services departments to handle these young people, but also as a political symbol that the government is getting tough on law and order.

But what is to be done about Borstal? If it were a business it would have had the receivers in years ago. Attempts at reform have failed, the expansion of the system must fail on an even bigger scale. The Borstals should be phased out. What do we put in its place? Ideas about alternatives abound, there are hundreds of latter day Alexander Pattersons who, if the political will existed, would get their alternatives going tomorrow. The thing which unites all these alternatives (e.g. community service orders, intermediate treatment, etc.) is that their reconviction rates are certainly no higher and most are considerably lower than the Borstal and they cause much less damage to the young people with whom they work. Common humanity, statistical evidence, and above all, common sense demand the abolition of the Borstal institution.

3f. Special Means of Control

Prison

Although there are many disturbing features of our present institutional treatment of children, 'shock' press reports have been particularly prompted by news that prison establishments, other than Borstals and detention centres, are being used to hold children under 17.

The majority of these children, both boys and girls, are placed within local prisons or remand centres on what is known as 'certificates of unruliness'. The 1969 Childen and Young Persons Act specifies that a court which remands someone under 17 in custody, i.e. not on bail, must turn him or her over to the local authority. However, if the court believes, usually on evidence provided by the local authority, that the child is 'unruly' he/she is then dispatched to a prison department establishments. Also, if a local authority at some point during the time a child is in care decides the child is 'unruly', it can apply to a court for

---

Children and Young Persons Received into Custody 1977

Detention Centres:
Senior   1166
Junior   1786
Borstals:
Closed   3728
Open   1685
Prisons: 540
This figure includes untried and convicted unsentenced males & females aged 14 to 20, plus 108 borstal trainees.

Remand Centres: 1576
This figure is made up of a similar population to those in prison.

Number of children & young persons detained under Section 53 of the Children and Young Persons Act 1933: 68 persons initially received on sentence — 10 were sentenced indefinitely although one appealed successfully; 10 sent to community homes; three to youth treatment centres; 28 to borstal; and 30 to young prisoner centres.
(All above figures from the Report on the Work of the Prison Department 1977 and the Prison Statistics 1977.)

From Prison Department Report (1977): '. . . in 1977 more than 25,000 young offenders under 21 years of whom 775 were female, were received into custody under sentence. This was an increase over 1976 of 4% for males and 8% for females.

'. . . the increase in receptions in recent years was partly due to the increasing number of 14 to 16 year olds coming before the courts, and partly to the increasing use by the courts of custodial sentences for persons in this age group.'

The overall increase between 1973 and 1977 of young persons received into custody was 41.42%. It is worth noting that the increase in 14 to 16 year olds proceeded against at magistrates courts between 1976 and 1977 was only 3.36%.

Receptions into Prison Department Establishments by Age and type of custody 1973-1977

AGE 14-15	1973 M	1973 F	1974 M	1974 F	1975 M	1975 F	1976 M	1976 F	1977 M	1977 F
Section 53 (1)	4	–	2	–	3	–	10	–	10	–
Section 53 (2)	41	1	22	1	36	3	45	2	56	2
Borstal	1159	49	1240	60	1449	84	1654	94	1703	79
Detention Centre	3062	–	3689	–	4378	–	4890	–	5228	–
Other	4	–								
TOTAL	4270	50	4953	61	5916	87	6599	96	6997	81

AGE 17-20	1973 M	1973 F	1974 M	1974 F	1975 M	1975 F	1976 M	1976 F	1977 M	1977 F
Fine default	1069	81	1512	98	1900	146	2063	158	2418	196
Immediate imprisonment	2417	109	2627	107	3275	148	3770	210	4276	230
Borstal	4639	207	4926	229	5777	315	5593	255	5200	268
Detention Centre	5048	–	5462	–	5825	–	5554	–	5635	–
TOTAL	13173	397	14527	434	16777	609	16980	623	17529	694
GRAND TOTALS	17443	447	19480	495	22693	696	23579	719	24526	775

(All figures except grand totals taken from Table 3.5 of *Prison Statistics 1977*)

the child to be remanded to a prison department establishment. It is these practices which are the cause of such press reports as, 'Children Behind Bars — The Scandal that Must End' (*Daily Mirror*, 10 May 1976).

The House of Commons Expenditure Committee found that, as of 1974, over 3,000 certificates of unruliness were issued annually, and the following statement was made: 'We condemn in the strongest possible terms the use of certificates of unruliness as a means of achieving secure accommodation. We recommend that the practice of remanding young persons to adult prisons must cease forthwith.'

Now, five years later, the Government is moving slowly towards ending this practice. For example, girls under 17 can no longer be remanded to prisons by this procedure. In addition, a tightening of the criteria for the issue of such certificates has meant a drop in the total numbers sent to prison.

But the suspicion that this improvement was more related to the pejorative connotations of the word 'prison' than to any careful assessment of the advantages of alternative regimes, was confirmed by the use of the prison issue to promote the establishment of more secure units. *The Times* of 14 May 1976 declared that: 'The solution cannot be found without the provision of substantial resources for the building of (or conversion of existing buildings into) secure homes.' The inadequacy of this solution is considered below.

Secure Units

There is probably no better example of the hypocrisies and inconsistencies which lie at the heart of much of the present system of juvenile justice in this country, than the story of the secure units. Few weeks pass without calls for more secure accommodation for the 'increasingly violent young offenders' and the right to commit young people directly to such institutions without the mediation of a social worker has become the major political demand of the Magistrates' Association. Indeed, the present Conservative Government's commitment to tough law and order policies might well have led them to concede this particular demand from the magistracy — but they were at least practical enough to recognise that there were simply not enough places at present available to satisfy the likely punitive demand.*

Paula is Freed from Holloway

The Mirror's campaign to stop children being sent to prison got off to a happy start.

The parents of Paula, the imprisoned 16 year old schoolgirl, were told yesterday that their daughter had been released from Holloway.

And as Parliamentary support for the campaign grew last night, Paula was *settling down in a Borstal.* (*Daily Mirror,* 11 May 1976, our italics).

Secure units are to be found in community homes with education, in observation and assessment centres and at the special youth treatment centres for disturbed children. Some are quite large and specially designed, others are merely locked rooms in a special part of the institution.

A recent DHSS report (Cawson and Martell, 1979) recounts some of their history, and documents the uneasy shift between claims about their rehabilitative advantages and their more straightforward punitive functions.

There has been a demand for closed or secure units for certain young offenders almost as long as there had been residential accommodation for young people. Those responsible at the Home Office for the old Approved Schools in the late 1950s were interested in some type of closed provision for children who ran away. A working party was set up in 1959 which suggested some form of closed school to deal with such persistent absconders. Their report had just been issued when trouble broke out at the Carlton Approved School. Although little damage or injury occurred during the trouble, it caused considerable consternation throughout the system, and was directly responsible for the establishment of another working party whose members included representatives from the Children's Department Inspectorate, the Association of Managers of Approved Schools, the Association of Headmasters, Headmistresses and Matrons, and other Home Office officials. Originally the brief was to look at the problems of (a) disturbed individuals, (b) those needing psychiatric care, and (c) the unruly and the absconders, but it was the last category which received most attention. The final report suggested the establishment of secure units at three schools to deal with such individuals. It is interesting to note, however, that submissions from both the Associations represented on the party did not

---

*Magistrate's powers will however be extended in 1980 so that they may insist upon a child being taken away from home.

think the idea of closed units was a good one. Instead they suggested separate places with specially trained staff to deal with the boys, rather than physical restraint: closed units they thought would only lead to disruptive behaviour. But punitive thinking prevailed, based largely on the notion that there were a few bad boys who were causing problems. If something were done with these 'rotten apples', especially something with a deterrent value, then the rest of the system would operate properly.

A 1967 review of the three units set up in the preceding three years discovered that the operation of the units was moving away from the original ideas behind their establishment. Instead of being used as secure units for short-term punishment, they had evolved into longer-range 'therapeutic' programmes. Frequently boys sent to the units stayed longer than six months, and might never be sent to their intended open school. The review argued that in certain cases, boys who were not a security problem might benefit from the supposed treatment facilities of a closed unit.

A further review took place in 1969 in line with the changes which were coming under the Children and Young Persons Act. This included discussion on the use of secure units for the severely disturbed, again emphasising the units' therapeutic value. In spite of the fact that there seemed to be some

---

'Naturally, one expects to see bars in a secure unit.

One also expects to hear the jangle of keys, but one prison feature we did not hope to find was the unlovely practice of slopping-out.

The units can offer no better symbol of the punitive and degrading perspectives that hovered at their birth than the morning row of chamber pots.

After all, plumbing had achieved a modest degree of sophistication in 1965 and slopping-out has since been deliberately avoided at two of the most recent secure units.

It seems incredible that regimes which seem to involve large numbers of staff for case conferences on boys' welfare cannot offer sufficient night supervision for boys to go to the lavatory in a civilised way.' (S. Millham *et al, Locking Up Children,* 1978.)

---

agreement between the Home Office and the schools operating the units on this function of the units, one school found it necessary to comment on how and when other schools were using its unit:

At present the only really firm criteria for transfer to the Special Unit seems to be that the boy makes an unmitigated nuisance of himself and there is no other alternative placing that could make people feel comfortable about his disposal. (Quoted in Cawson and Martell, 1979)

By 1971, the DHSS had responsibility for the secure units within the new Community Homes system. The Department's discussion paper on the *Development of Secure Provision in Community Homes* indicates that the treatment ethic had now emerged as the most acceptable rationale for secure units. Basically, the paper made clear that the use of the secure unit as a place to send

Nightmare world of a young girl

Jane's nightmare began when she was 12 years old, and ended two years later when she was released from her youth treatment centre. She still bears the mental and physical scars of her time at St Charles, in Brentwood, Essex.

Jane is 17 years old, settled down with a job and a London flat, although she is technically in care. Her imprisonment ended three years ago, but it was clearly still painful to talk about it. She was locked up after four years of petty stealing, and running away from children's homes. Her father was in prison, and Jane kept having arguments with her mother over her affair with another man.

'When I went to St Charles, they told me I'd be there for just a few weeks. I had to strip off and they searched me,' she began.

'On the second day I was there, one girl held me down and I was tattooed by other kids — and the staff did nothing about it.'

She showed me the scars on her arms where she later had the tattoos — made with ink and a needle — surgically removed.

In spite of the security, the high inmate-staff ratio and the constant supervision, Jane was later stabbed by another girl.

'To calm me down,' she said, 'they put me in a padded room with the lights out. I was kept there in the dark for three days with just a coarse army blanket. I just can't describe what it was like.'

Her daily routine began at 7.30 when the bedroom doors were unlocked, one by one. There were six girls and six boys in her unit. The bed and the wardrobe were securely fixed so they couldn't be moved and some of the bedrooms had a sink.

'The water was lukewarm so you couldn't scald yourself and there was no plug, and the water just dribbled out. There was a little glass window in the door so they could look in. There was no keyhole or anything. The door was locked on the outside. You'd go to the bathroom to wash, but there were no locks there either, and anybody could just walk in.'

After breakfast — the meals were sent into the unit on a trolley — there was a study period, then after the midday meal the inmates were taken to their bedrooms and locked up again. 'The staff called it "siesta", and said it was for us to let our food digest. But I think it was really just for their convenience.'

They were unlocked at 3 o'clock for another study period, and they were later allowed to watch television until the trolley arrived with their tea. After tea, it was 'leisure time' until they went to bed at 8 or 9 o'clock, depending, said Jane, on how well they'd behaved during the day.

'There was a bell in the room you had to ring if you wanted to be released to go to the toilet, but a couple of the kids had potties, and had to slop-out in the morning.'

That was the routine for months on end.

'After a year I got out down to the shops with the host worker at weekends. The host worker was the member of staff who was like your personal social worker. Mobility meant you were only allowed out with your host worker. "Full mobility" was when you were allowed out with other members of staff.'

One of the worst aspects of the treatment was the psychological games the staff would exercise on the young inmates.

'There would be a group meeting every Thursday afternoon, and there would be 12 members of staff firing off down on one small kid. There was this little kid, only 12 years old. And he was incontinent. They tried to crack him up and get him going. We couldn't match them with our experience. You just got mangled in the end and didn't know what you were doing. They would move us on from one situation to another. They knew how to make kids laugh and how to make them cry. They were playing psychological games with us.'

She said there was a feeling that they'd never get out of the place. 'Kids', she concluded, 'shouldn't be allowed to go through that. These places shouldn't be allowed to exist.' (*Labour Weekly* 24 August 1979.)

---

someone as a 'last resort' was not appropriate. Instead, the units were to be seen as an acceptable alternative form of treatment.

Today there are approximately 400 secure places variously used for treatment or punishment, or both, depending on which rationale is in vogue at the moment. But whatever rationale prevails, the emphasis is upon the faults or problems of the individual. That is, the behaviour which has led someone to be referred to a unit is assumed to have originated entirely from within the individual and be unrelated to the nature of institutional life. It should follow from this, for example, that if a particular Community school has a group of disruptive boys, then their removal will result in greater success after discharge for those from the same institution. Such is not the case. Rather, it seems that places which have a high rate of referral to secure units also have a high reconviction rate among those who are discharged. In other words, institutions themselves seem to have a profound effect on the behaviour of those who go to secure units. Indeed, the research by Millham *et al* (1978) and in Cawson and Martell (1979) establishes that it was not the individuals' offence backgrounds which provided the major

---

Secure Places

'At 1 June 1979, there were 244 long-term and 126 short-term security places in community homes in England and Wales. A total of 54 long-term and 116 short-term places are under construction and a further eight long-term and 49 short-term places are planned.

In addition, the Department has provided and administers two youth treatment centres. 12 of the 32 places at St Charles youth treatment centre, Brentwood, are secure and a further 12 secure places are planned. Glenthorpe youth treatment centre, Birmingham, when fully operational, will provide 54 secure places; 20 are currently occupied.' (Sir George Young. House of Commons reply.)

reason for their eventual referral to a secure unit. Despite the suggestion that more violent offences against the person are being committed by juveniles (p.3 of the Joint Working Party of the Magistrates Association, Association of Metropolitan Authorities and the Association of County Councils *Report* 1978), these 'extra-mural' violent children did not seem to be represented in the secure unit population. Although some had undoubtedly been involved in violence, this had actually occurred not outside but within the institution. In fact a fifth of the children in secure accommodation, including the majority of girls, had never been taken to court following an offence.

The presence of children with a record of institutional violence in the units makes one wonder how a more secure environment, i.e. a further restriction of freedom, is going to reduce this type of behaviour?

> *There is no justification for the belief which underlay so many referrals that the child who was violent in care would become dangerous to the outside community.* This cannot be said too broadly or too often. The results suggested completely the reverse: that the violence, where it occurred was generated by institutional situation and would be more likely to increase than decrease in a more restrictive setting. (Cawson and Martell, 1979.)

As we have suggested a major argument for the expansion of secure units rests on the idea that young people referred to Community Homes with Education facilities (CHEs) are more difficult than in the past: more secure provisions are therefore necessary to cope with this increase. More units in fact are already on their way: information prepared in August 1978 by the DHSS indicated that the number of secure places planned or under construction would be more than the existing number of places. Yet the research of Millham *et al* (1978) and Cawson and Martell (1979) does not indicate a more difficult group of children entering the system. Indeed, the latter researchers suggest that because greater numbers of older and more difficult juveniles are being sent to borstal, those in the child care system may even be less difficult than in the past.

Millham *et al*, after a careful study of the backgrounds of a sample of children in secure units, reached the following conclusion:

> We cannot see . . . any aspects of the boys' backgrounds that would lead to suggest that there has been any marked change in the quality of boys coming into CHEs or to justify any demand for an extension of secure provision (p.46) . . . There is no evidence that boys in today's CHEs are more difficult or, in terms of likely recidivism, at greater risk than in previous years. If such reasons are advanced to justify an increase in secure places, they are misplaced. (Millham *et al*, 1978)

It is also relevant to note that certain areas of the England and Wales have few or no secure places in CHEs (although all areas seem to have at least one in an observation and assessment centre). Yet such areas seem able to cope adequately without them.

Appalled Staff Member

'The whole atmosphere was frightening', was how one former member of staff described his stint at an assessment centre.

Bill — who doesn't want his full identity disclosed — was appalled at the staff's attitude to the boys and girls.

'The whole regime is designed to irritate and attack the kids. They were always wound up by the staff. Most of my work was outside the secure unit, and even in those most open conditions, things were pretty disheartening. One senior staff member gratuitously smashed one boy's face into the wall. Another kept referring to half-cast kids as "sambo" and generally meted out pretty rough treatment. On a camping trip, one girl was stripped and hosed down in front of the staff and other boys and girls. The staff were always indulging in humiliating treatment of the weak. The regime itself therefore encouraged violent behaviour.' (*Labour Weekly* 24 August 1979.)

So what are the remaining justifications for the units? The old notion that security was somehow a way to dissipate aggression seems to have disappeared from view. The 1971 DHSS paper on secure provision did talk of the units as providing an opportunity for the reduction of aggression by 'acting out' but research has shown that this is unlikely to be effective. (Sinclair, Tizard and Clarke, 1971).

The DHSS in the circular to local authorities on secure accommodation was somewhat vague as to what a secure unit was to do beyond accommodating 'needs which staff cannot meet unless supplied with the additional facility of physical security . . .' The aim of the treatment 'is to enable them to move from a state of imposed control to one of self-control' (Local Authority Circular 75). The circular continues:

'In a secure unit, the first essential of the arrangement is continuous and effective control. Further essentials are flexibility and the encouragement of creative ability . . . A special emphasis on creative ability is required to counteract the frustration which a physically restricted environment must tend to produce, and which lends to disruptive behaviour or passivity.'

Here, the stress is on control, yet other activities are encouraged as it is recognised that the control will produce frustration and possibly disruptive behaviour. But, according to Millham *et al*, the units have not done amazingly well in terms of providing creative outlets. In fact, the contrary seems to be the case. They conclude that '. . . in general, the organisational priorities of security and the educational emphasis seem to elbow care areas aside.'

Whatever it is that secure units are meant to be doing, they do not appear to be reducing reoffending by those who pass through the units. Researchers seem to differ only on the ways in which the units do not work, while generally agreeing that they are ineffective. Millham *et al's* sample indicated that only 24% of those released from the units did not reoffend: '. . . secure accommodation is

79

no more successful in modifying behaviour than were the CHEs of our earlier study'. On the other hand, the DHSS research found that experience in a secure unit actually increased the chance of reoffending for younger children or those who had not committed offences prior to going in. In the case of those who had offended several times in the past, being in a secure unit did not appear to have made any difference.

The issue frequently side-stepped or glossed over is that of the rights of the child who is put into the units. Confusion exists over whether he/she is there as a punishment, for treatment, or both, or even neither (e.g. no other suitable place is available). And while a child may have the right of appeal against a care order, there is no right of appeal against the type of disposition instituted after the care order is made. It seems somewhat contradictory to allow an appeal against a committal to a detention centre or a Borstal, but not against placement in a secure unit, particularly when the regime in such a unit may be even more restrictive than that in a detention centre or Borstal, and be applied for the same punitive reasons.

Drugs

The story of the increased use of medication to control children in institutions is necessarily incomplete. Details of the type of drugs used and of the regularity of their use are simply not available. The DHSS says that the drugging of children is a matter for doctors' clinical judgement, and admits that it has no idea how many children are drugged, and that it has never tried to find out how many doses of tranquilizers are prescribed every year for children. The picture is very much like that to be found in the adult prison system. Occasionally a conscientious member of staff or a concerned inmate will report some obvious malpractices and this will be immediately followed by massive denials by the concerned authorities. Dr Masud Hoghugi, the Principal of Aycliffe School, has pointed to the possible scale of the abuse and the reasons why it may have failed to become a cause for concern.

> Chemical agents of various forms can be used to minimise the risk presented by a person to others. A youngster who is 'tranquilized' does not attack other people, one who is put to sleep does not escape or commit offences. The use of medication as an aid to control is more widespread and often more indiscriminate and unjustified than is commonly realised. It does not, however, arouse the same strong emotions in the public as 'secure accommodation' because it is administered in a medical setting, which is presumably concerned with a healing process and by people who should know what they are doing. (*Community Care*, 28 September 1977.)

One of the problems of monitoring the 'indiscriminate and unjustified' use of drugs described by Hoghugi is the growth of private children's homes. which are not even subject to formal DHSS inspection.* These homes freely advertise for

*The Government has recently decided not to proceed with legislation which would have ensured the inspection of such homes.

'clients' in social work journals and in some cases specialise in dealing with difficult and disturbed children. The most recent reports of drug abuse on the files at MIND concern just such a private children's home in the south of England. The complaints came from a group of social workers and from a superintendent of an assessment centre, and both concerned 13 year old girls who had been placed in the home by different local authorities. The drugs involved were major tranquillizers which are mainly prescribed to counter psychotic behaviour and which have been referred to as the 'chemical cosh' in view of their tendency to induce a 'lifeless' or 'shocked' state. The super-intendent told us:

> We had had this kid with us for a year before she was sent to B Lodge. She was a very difficult but likeable 12 year old. She was placed in B Lodge because none of our children's homes were prepared to take her. Last Christmas she came back to the assessment centre for the holiday. When she arrived we were absolutely stunned to see the difference in her. She was little more than a "zombie". She had been placed on a heavy dosage of major tranquillizers and had been on them for the year that she spent at B Lodge. When I saw here I immediately called in our own psychiatrist, who agreed that she should be taken off the drugs. I then rang the superintendent of B Lodge to explain this and express my concern. I later learned that my Director of Social Services had written behind my back to apologise for my actions. The girl is now back with us full time and is as disturbed and difficult as she was before but at least she has a personality.

The delegation of social workers who came to see MIND about the same children's home also spoke of major tranquillizers being used on another 13 year old girl. When an attempt was made to enquire further into the case the investigation was stopped by the Director of Social Services on the grounds, we were later informed, that if the girl were thrown out of B Lodge the Department would not be able to find an alternative placement for her. The private home in question is well known to senior officials in the DHSS who informed the authors that existing legislation gave them no right to intervene, although moves were being made in the Department to rectify this situation.

Local authority homes may be more open to scrutiny than the newly-emerging private institutions, but there is no shortage of evidence that they too rely upon medication as a form of long-term social control rather than for the treatment of specific symptions. MIND runs a residential project for instituationalised young-sters and regularly finds that candidates for admission have been on long-term prescriptions of major tranquillizers. One of the present residents had been on Modecate, a major tranquillizer, for five years prior to his admission. The original prescription was made when he was in an assessment centre and he continued to receive fortnightly injections (the 'advantage' of drugs like Modecate is that they need to be administered so infrequently) throughout his institutional career until the staff of the MIND project and their consultant psychiatrist weaned him off the substance over a period of 12 months. This had to be done in the face of strong opposition from the psychiatrist who had originally prescribed the drug. After the drug had been discontinued there was no evidence of the 'psychotic

> Drugs are being widely used by staff in institutions to control difficult children. This is the result of a *Community Care* investigation which came to four major conclusions.
>
> Drugs are being used to sedate difficult children, without any specific treatment in mind.
>
> There is broad agreement that the use of drugs is acceptable for the treatment of identified mental illnesses or abnormalities which cause bad behaviour.
>
> There is professional disagreement between those involved in child care as to when it is permissible to use drugs to control problem children when there is no evidence of psychological causes.
>
> The use of drugs purely to control children may in fact be illegal.
> (*Community Care,* 4 October 1979.)

symptoms' which would have provided the only justification for the initial prescription of the drug.

Probably the most dramatic statement about present trends was made earlier this year by Dr Colin Brewer, a consultant psychiatrist at a girls' assessment centre (quoted in *Labour Weekly*, 24 August 1979):

> These days some staff would rather stick a needle in a child's backside than impose sanctions on them like loss of liberty or money. What should be worrying us is that some children are being given big doses with unpleasant side effects for months at a time. Using drugs in this way is often a reflection of bad management. It's difficult to see how they're supposed to learn to behave better if they are kept like zombies for long periods.

MIND was recently able to obtain some statements which confirm Dr Brewer's comments on the readiness to resort to drugs for control. A member of staff at a southern adolescent unit declared:

> We only give drugs when we're anxious . . . say if an adolescent comes in here and smashes my office up, I'll sedate him . . . We say 'I'm giving you this to give me a break' . . . Conventional psychiatric hospitals deal with people by giving them chemotheraphy and ECT and all those sort of things. My belief is that they give them for the same reasons that we give drugs here — because they can't cope.

What should surely be worrying us rather more than the news that 'some children are being given big doses with unpleasant side effects for months at a time' is that there is absolutely no procedure by which the child or his parents or their representatives are able to register their objections to such medication. The drugs are prescribed as part of the treatment, even as 'in the child's interests'. Adult prisoners who are drugged as a form of social control may at least have friends inside who are able to articulate their concern, or they may be able to communicate their own anxieties. They may even know what drugs they are being prescribed and have some ability to recognise their side effects. How much more frightening must their impact be upon the inarticulate, unsophisticated, isolated child.

Even those who protest their innocence over this question of long-term enforced medication are able in the present state of affairs to talk in terms of it being a personal choice that they have decided to make, rather than a necessity forced upon them by an acknowledgement of children's rights, or subscription to a code of professional conduct. Thus we find the Director of St Charles Youth Treatment Centre commendably declaring his opposition to sedation, but not in terms of any universal consideration: it just happens to be his Centre's policy, and as such could no doubt change depending upon an administrative or 'therapeutic' whim:

> Drugs are rarely used, partly because children with a serious diagnosis of mental illness, like schizophrenia, would not be accepted. However, having seen how disturbed the children can be, especially in their acting out, the psychiatrist expressed his surprise that more were not under sedation, as they would have been in any hospital. But the centre's policy is to use good child techniques rather than medication. A child is taken off any tranquillizers when he is admitted, after consultation with the psychiatrist and medical officer because we want to see the real child. (Lindsay Knight, *Community Care*, 31 March 1976.)

The reference to taking children off 'tranquillizers' is presumably a reference to the sedation policy pursued in other children's institutions and not to the children's 'extra-mural' drug habits, in that those who are admitted to St Charles Youth Treatment Centre have invariably had previous institutional experience. The Director in the same article referred to 'one boy, who had been in 18 institutions in only two years'.

There is a faint hope that the Conservative Government may be prepared to do something about this disturbing state of affairs. At least they cannot deny all knowledge of the problem. The present Health Minister, Dr Gerard Vaughan, admitted earlier this year (when in opposition) that:

> There is no doubt now that drugs are abused when there is a shortage of staff, or few trained staff. I'm afraid that far too often drugs are given to a child, not for his own sake but simply to quieten him down. This year, the Year of the Child — a long hard look should be taken at how we treat our problem children. (quoted in *Labour Weekly*, 24 August 1979.)

Drugs and Consent

A particularly interesting feature in this situation is that under common law, a child is regarded (subject only to his ability to comprehend the nature of the proposed treatment) to be competent to give an informed consent for medical treatment. Thus a child may have a legal right to refuse to be placed under 'chemical control'. Larry Gostin, an international authority on the subject, summarised the legal position as follows:

The current statutory position in England is that the consent of a minor who has attained the age of 16 to medical or dental treatment which, in the absence of consent would constitute a trespass to the person, is effective as if the minor were of full age (Family Law Reform Act 1969 Section 8). This legislation does not, however, revoke any common law right of a minor below the age of 16 to consent on his own behalf. In this regard the preferred view is that a minor's competency depends upon whether he or she can comprehend what is involved in the procedure in question; *there are no fixed rules based upon age, legal status or medical condition.* (Gostin, 1979, our italics.)

Whether those children in care who are prescribed major tranquillizers or sedatives to control their behaviour have given their consent or not is not known. We very strongly doubt it, just as we doubt that they or their parents have even been consulted in any meaningful way. If, as the evidence seems to suggest, these children have been 'medicated' without their informed consents (i.e. subject only to a prior determination of their ability to comprehend the treatment involved), their common law rights have been breached. Furthermore, it would appear from Gostin's exposition of the law that those responsible for administering these drugs may be liable to civil actions for assault against the children involved. However, a legal right is only meaningful if the child involved knows of its existence *and* the means by which that right can be enforced. Equally an informed consent to treatment is only valid if such a child knows that he has an enforceable right to refuse it.

4

Conclusions and Recommendations

In this section we endeavour to suggest a number of ways in which the various denials of natural justice and rights which we have encountered in the text, might be remedied. We have found ourselves primarily drawing upon American resources in this respect. This is no accident. For following the 1967 Gault decision in that country which held that juveniles charged with delinquency and facing possible incarceration are constitutionally entitled to notice, counsel, confrontation, cross examination and the privilege against self-incrimination — there has been an extended and sophisticated debate about the principle issues at stake.

Apart from our general prescriptions for increasing natural justice in the processing and institutionalisation of children, we also include a number of more specific recommendations derived from our examination of particular elements within the present system.

4a. Standards for Juvenile Justice

(These proposals are based upon the reforms outlined by the American Juvenile Justice Standards Project — a joint undertaking of the American Bar Association and the Institute of Judicial Administration. We have taken into account the most valuable comments made upon this enterprise by a British commentator, Morris 1978).

1. *Sanctions for juveniles should be proportional to the seriousness of the offences which they have committed.* The Justice Standards Project proposes a specific tariff but the details of this are rather less important than the general point that all sanctions (whether they specify secure facilities or probation) are ordered for a specific period of time. In this country, such a principle would mean that length of stay in, say, a detention centre was directly compared to length of stay in an assessment centre or community home, and both then allotted an appropriate place within the tariff system.

2. *Sentences or dispositions should be determinate.* This undermines one of the principal characteristics of juvenile 'sentences' in this country — their indeterminacy. Children sent to community homes, assessment centres, and

Borstals as a result of an offence (whether or not this is connected to 'welfare' considerations) have no way of knowing their exact date of release — or to put it another way — the actual length of their sentence.

3. *The court should choose the least restrictive category and duration of disposition that is appropriate to the seriousness of the offence.* This is not a criterion which plays a major part in our juvenile court proceedings, particularly as it is rare for there to be anyone on hand in court who could testify about the actual duration of possible sentences or the degree of restrictiveness they might represent. The further declaration in the American standards that dispositions should not be imposed unless the necessary resources exist would presumably provide the legal representatives of children and parents with the opportunity to question the 'assessment' which occurred in 'assessment' centres, the 'training' in Borstals, and the quality of 'education' in Community Homes with 'education'.

4. *Non-criminal misbehaviour such as running away from home and victimless offences such as marijuana and alcohol use and consensual sexual behaviour should be removed from the jurisdiction of the juvenile court.* Voluntary programmes within the community are suggested as alternatives.

Some notion of the effect of this change upon our present system can be gauged from the total of children committed to care under section 1 (2) (e) of the Children and Young Persons Act which deals with truancy, and section 1(2) (c) which covers 'moral danger'. (In practice, this last category is almost invariably concerned with 'promiscuous' girls. A senior social worker could not recall a single case in his career in which the concept 'promiscuous' had been applied to a boy.) The most recent figures for these categories (1977) are:

Section 1 (2) (e)   1,100
Section 1 (2) (c)   200

5. *The limitation of discretion in the processing of juveniles. Formal criteria are laid down for referrals at each stage of the proceedings, such that police, for example, have no choice but to refer juveniles accused of minor offences to youth service agencies which provide a variety of services on a voluntary basis.*

This removal of discretion from the police in such cases would do much to remove the anomalies referred to in section 2 (d) above.

6. *There is a right to legal representation for all interested parties (that is, parents as well as juveniles) at all critical stages in the proceedings.* This is in direct contrast with the situation described in our section 2 (c). We are aware of the logistic problems that are posed by such an extension of legal representation and would be prepared to modify this demand by recommending that, at least initially, representation of the child should be confined to all those cases in which there was a possibility of institutional commitment being recommended.

7. *Once the category and duration of the disposition have been determined by the judge (magistrate) the choice of a particular programme should be governed by the needs and desires of the individual.*

As we indicated in section 2 (c) there are few occasions in which the juvenile meaningfully participates in court proceedings in this country: the idea that he/she might directly determine the outcome by his/her own wishes (as distinct from the social worker's interpretation of these wishes) is rarely considered.

8. *Limitations on intervention prior to adjudication and disposition.* The intention here is to make decision-makers release juveniles after arrest and before 'sentence' or to justify not having done so. Such a provision would make large inroads into the number of juveniles remanded in care for reports, and of course dramatically reduce the number who are sent to prisons and remand centres before facing court proceedings.

It is fair to point out that Allison Morris detects within these principles a commitment to notions associated with punishment — proportionally, determinacy and objectivity — without any explicit discussion of such matters. Similarly, the authors of the standards appear to retain some commitment to the idea of treatment. But when such standards are measured against the concept of natural justice, and contrasted with the present procedures in this country, it is difficult not to concur with her eventual verdict that 'despite their faults (they) demand serious consideration in the development of a rational juvenile justice policy.' (Morris 1978)

4b. Grounds for Intervention

The standards for juvenile justice which we have just outlined relate primarily to juveniles who have been charged with specific criminal offences. This leaves out of account the large numbers of juveniles who are brought before our courts, on the grounds that although they have committed no specific offence, they are in need of care and protection for any of the various reasons outlined in section 2 (a).

In this book, we do not specifically wish to elaborate upon questions of whether such individual should in fact appear before the juvenile court as at present constituted or before some other panel. We should say, however, that we detect considerable advantages from the point of view of natural justice in the recent suggestion by Priestley *et al* (1977) that children suffering from parental neglect or abuse should be dealt with by entirely separate court jurisdiction.

But whatever the administrative tribunal which might be established in this area, we would still be faced with the need for clear criteria to determine who should appear before it. Something very much more consistent and coherent than the present criteria seems to be demanded if natural justice is to be served. The following proposals based upon a formulation by Michael S. Wald, Professor of Law at Stanford University (in Rosenheim, 1976) would do much to resolve the ambiguities and arbitrariness which at present exist within our care procedures. In particular, their reliance upon 'harm' as distinct from 'conduct' would dramatically reduce the impact of the dubious family pathology model which as we have seen in section 2 (b) lies behind so many of our present care proceedings.

1. Coercive societal intervention should be premised upon specific harms to a child, not on the basis of parental conduct.
2. Only the following categories of harm should be admitted:

a. A child is suffering or there is substantial likelihood that he or she will imminently suffer a serious injury and

b. Where the intervention will not create a greater harm than that which led to the intervention.

3. Harms for which intervention is permitted.

a. A child has suffered a non-accidental physical injury causing disfigurement, impairment of bodily functioning or severe bodily harm, or there is a substantial likelihood that the child will imminently suffer such an injury.

b. A child is suffering serious emotional damage evidenced by severe anxiety, depression or withdrawal, and his/her parents are unwilling/unable to provide or permit the necessary treatment for him/her.

c. A child has been sexually abused by a member of his/her household.

d. A child is in need of medical treatment to present serious physical harm and his/her parents and are unwilling/unable to provide or permit the necessary treatment for him/her.

4c. Charter of Rights for Children in Institutions

This charter of rights draws upon three principal sources: the Council of Europe's Resolution 77 (33) on the placement of children (adopted on 3 November 1977), a text prepared by MIND as a statute for formal admission to, and discharge from, a treatment facility, and a document 'Declaration of the Rights of the Child' drawn up by a *Voice of the Child in Care* Working Party.

1. All residents shall have the right to dignity, privacy and humane care: each institution will ensure that each resident may live as normally as possible: each resident should have the right to be fully informed as to his legal status.

2. Each resident shall have the right to:

    i. receive sealed correspondence.

    ii. send correspondence unopened, and have access to writing materials, postage and staff assistance where necessary.

    iii. send and receive confidential telephone calls.

    iv. receive visitors at any time during the day.

    v. make visits outside the institution.

    vi. have access to facilities and equipment for physical exercise.

    vii. go out of doors daily.

    viii. keep and use personal possessions, including their own clothes.

    ix. communicate and interact with persons of their own choice, including members of the opposite sex, upon the consent of such persons.

    x. have access to individually locked storage space for their private use.

    xi. keep and spend an amount of money equivalent to that available to one of similar age and status outside the institution.

    xii. receive any financial benefits which might be available outside the institution (e.g. supplementary benefit).

    xiii. receive the same educational opportunities as other children outside the institution.

    xiv. receive a nutritious and varied diet, and have an opportunity to purchase and experiment with the cooking and eating of foods.

xv. independent medical examination.

xvi. contraception and, if necessary, abortion services on the same basis as other young people in the community.

xvii. know what punishments and sanctions are permitted in the place where they live; and to know what the rules are and what may happen if they break them.

xviii. access by themselves or by their parents or representatives to all documents pertaining to themselves.

xix. three-monthly review of 'sentence' or 'treatment' (except in the case of regimes with determinate sentences).

xx. participate, or have parents or representatives, participate in decisions taken by the review body.

xxi. refer their own case after review to independent body at which they, or their parents or representatives, will participate.

xxii. subject only to a prior determination of the child's ability to comprehend the factors involved, the right to give informed consent to, or to refuse treatment, particularly treatments which are hazardous, irreversible, experimental or unproven.

xxiii. refuse to be moved from a place where they wish to stay without a conference, independently chaired, at which they are present or represented.

The charter below was drawn up by a group of young people in care.

Charter of rights for young people in care

We have drawn up this charter for 'young people' because we feel it is the responsibility of the residential worker and social worker to make sure that younger kids get a good deal.

1. The right to be accepted and treated as an individual member of society. Also the right to be treated with the same respect given to any other valid member of the human race.

2. The right to know who we are. To know our parents and brothers and sisters. To have factual information about our family origins and background.

3. The right to be able to make our own decisions and to have real influence over those decisions we are sometimes considered too thick to participate in.

4. The right to privacy. We understand that in care it is not always possible to choose who we are going to live and share our lives with. But we are still human beings and are still entitled to the essential amount of privacy needed before cracking up.

5. The right to be given an insight into the use of money by handling it,

using it and paying the consequences if we misuse it, e.g. being given the money in our hand to buy the clothes our clothing allowance will allow.

6. The right to choose those who will represent us whether it be legally or otherwise, e.g. social workers. Also the right to choose those whom we wish to confide in.

7. Finally, the right to be as much a part of society as the next person and not to be labelled in any way. In short, to live.

These rights can be interpreted how you like. But don't misuse them or distort them for your own devices. (From *Who Cares: Young People in Care Speak Out.* National Children's Bureau. 1977.)

4d. Some Specific and Immediate Recommendations

Although we regard the juvenile justice system in this country as fundamentally flawed, we have no grounds for believing that it is likely to be reformed in any major way in the immediate future. The history of change in this area is not, as we emphasised in our introduction, one in which contradictions are resolved, irrationalities corrected, denials of natural justice remedied, or degrees of efficacy evaluated. Instead it is a record of compromise and expediency, in which the vested interests of the particular groups involved — magistrates, social workers, police, community home staff, prison department personnel — do more to determine the procedural and institutional outcome than any theoretical formulations or research findings.

It is for this reason that we also include in this section a set of very specific recommendations which, while not altering the nature of the present system, would do something to reduce its more glaring inconsistencies, and would also go some way to 'calling the bluff' on certain ideas and practices which do much to bolster the present state of affairs.

1. *Extension of the use of the caution to cases which at present lead to court appearances: the reduction of the present differences between police authorities in the employment of this procedure.*

This recommendation is aimed at increasing our tolerance of delinquency, at showing that society will not fall apart if even larger numbers of children who have committed relatively minor offences are dealt with outside the court. Some police authorities have already made a good start in this direction, although, as we have seen, the 'cautioning zeal' of Juvenile Bureaux may do something to invalidate this effect in certain areas. In addition, there is evidence that the police have been unofficially responsible, by the use of 'no further action' and cautionary procedures, for the relative rarity with which offenders between the age of 10-12 appear in court. The age of criminal responsibility has thus in effect been shifted upwards in line with the original hopes of the sponsors of the 1969 Act.

We might couple with this recommendation the idea which emerges from our consideration of the traffic paradox in section 2d, namely an increased reliance upon fines and a decreased dependence upon social enquiry reports in those relatively minor cases of delinquency which are not kept out of court by the use of cautions and 'no further action' decisions.

2. *The abolition or re-labelling of assessment centres in recognition of their actual functions as 'holding' or 'containment centres'.*

As we have argued in section 3a it is doubtful if anything which might meaningfully be called 'assessment' is occurring in those centres which enjoy the name. Not only does their present title provide our present ad hoc system of placement with a spurious scientific gloss, but it also conceals from the view of magistrates, parents, children and the general public, that we already possess a considerable number of establishments in which children who are supposedly in care, are in fact merely being 'warehoused'.

3. *A halt to the construction of 'secure units': immediate examination of the role of the existing units in view of research indicating that many 'problems' with which they cope are institutionally induced.*

Such an action might go some way to dealing with the myth that there is an alarming rise in the number of children whose behaviour is such as to require secure conditions. It is this belief which adds fuel to so many of the recent debates about juvenile justice.

We do not deny that there are certain children whose behaviour constitutes a serious threat to the safety or well-being of other people. However, as research indicates this number is smaller than assumed and might best be handled as suggested by Priestley *et al* by a new kind of public protection proceedings in the Crown Court. A protective custody order would commit the child to secure accommodation for a finite period and could be appealed or reviewed at three monthly intervals. This might act as some break upon the readiness of magistrates to detect dangerousness where none existed as well as ensuring that our debate about the juvenile justice system and about allocation of resources within it was not dominated by the regular introduction of this issue.

4. *An immediate enquiry into the use of medication for the purposes of control in juvenile institutions.* Such an enquiry would seek to establish the types of drugs which are at present administered, their differential use by institutions and the length of time for which they are prescribed.

5. *The implementation of the recommendation of the 1969 CYPA that Borstals should now be phased out.*

As section 3f indicates, there is now little credibility which can be attached to the idea of Borstals as offering some form of specialised treatment or training facilities (even though the Home Office handbook still manages to refer to a borstal sentence as 'the only form of medium term training for young offenders who need a longer period of remedial treatment than is available in detention centres'). The present punitive climate in this country might not allow their physical destruction (in fact £20m is at the moment being spent on rebuilding Feltham Borstal) but it would do much to remove a further source of hypocrisy from our juvenile justice system and possibly place some check on the court's readiness to recommend then, if they were relabelled 'prisons'. Such a relabelling might also put an end to the indeterminate Borstal sentence and prevent inmates from being troubled by members of staff who subscribe to some version of the 'treatment ethic'.

6. *The establishment of a Care and Control Test for all children subject to 7 (7) care orders which included the criteria agreed between Thorpe* et al *(1969) and senior child care officers.* That is (a) that the child should present a danger to himself or the community; (b) that he should have no home to go to — literally, or in the sense that family pressures make life at home intolerable; (c) that he should have medical, educational or psychological needs that can only be met in an institution.

We are aware that this recommendation, which would drastically reduce the number of young offenders at present being sent to institutions (see section 3d), is not fully compatible with our section on standards in juvenile justice. Nevertheless, in line with our argument at the beginning of this section, we believe that this is the type of recommendation which might do much to bring home some of the more outstanding inconsistencies within our present system of juvenile justice.

7. *The establishment of a National Children's Legal Centre.*

Although MIND and the National Council for Civil Liberties have frequently concerned themselves with a number of issues raised in this text (for example, with failures to observe standards of natural justice in courtroom procedures, and with the denial of children's rights in institutions) it is clearly impossible for them to monitor the whole range of abuses of natural justice and denial of rights to which we have drawn attention.

They are also faced with the problem of providing 'expert witnesses' to counter the claims made by social workers, psychologists, psychiatrists and institutional staff. The provision of legal representation alone as we have seen in our discussion of courtroom procedures is frequently not enough to counter 'best interests' arguments put forward by professional social workers who enjoy the support of the magistracy. Neither can lawyers be expected to argue effectively against the institutionalisation of children unless they have detailed evidence from expert witnesses about the unlikelihood of the institution in question being able to provide any better provision than that which is at present available in the community.

It is for these reasons that we welcome the possibility of a National Children's Legal Centre which might provide a resource for advice agencies, lawyers, children and parents.

Ideally such a centre should not be content with a passive role — for example, the provision of expert witnesses and legal representation when this is required — but should also actively seek out injustices in all parts of the system and attempt to remedy them through a series of test cases. Obvious candidates for such attention would be allocation to secure units, the use of medication for social control, the denial of justice and basic rights to handicapped, educationally subnormal and maladjusted children. Where general principles of civil liberty are raised then the centre should obviously co-operate with organisations like the NCCL.

The centre might be most effective if it were allied in some way with the creation of a Children's Ombudsman as proposed some years ago by NCCL and Justice. For the difficulty in safeguarding children's rights is that they, unlike adults, are not readily able to initiate complaints, or to know of the existence of an organisation which might remedy them. The centre then might engage in initial investigations and where no obvious legal remedy appeared available, pass the matter to an Ombudsman who would have the necessary powers to enquiry more fully into the matter and make an adjudication.

We are aware of the difficulties involved in creating an independent system of inspection and control, particularly in those areas where other forms of external inspection already exist. But we are not satisfied that the local authority and its social workers are the ideal groups to comment upon arrangements which they have often helped to initiate and are involved in administering. Neither are we convinced that managers, boards of governors, and boards of visitors who are supposed to constitute an independent external presence at other institutions, have in the past, adequately demonstrated an ability to keep their own viewpoint at all times separate from that of those involved in the day-to-day administration of the establishment.

5

Organisations

Apart from the National Council for Civil Liberties, the Cobden Trust and MIND the following organisations have taken a direct interest in many of the issues raised in this book.

FAMILY RIGHTS GROUP
24 Rommilly Road
London N4

JUSTICE FOR CHILDREN
35 Wellington Street
London WC1

NATIONAL CHILDREN'S BUREAU
8 Wakely Street
London EC1

ADVISORY CENTRE FOR EDUCATION (ACE)
18 Victoria Park Square
London E2

NATIONAL COUNCIL FOR ONE PARENT FAMILIES
255 Kentish Town Road
London NW5

VOICE OF THE CHILD IN CARE
60 Carysfort Road
London N8

A useful guide to children's legal rights has recently been published by NCCL. This is *First Rights* by Maggie Rae, Patricia Hewitt and Barry Hugill. Available from NCCL, price 85p.

6

Selected Bibliography

Anderson, Richard (1978) *Representation in the Juvenile Court.* Routledge and Kegan Paul.

Bean, Philip (1976) *Rehabilitation and Deviance.* Routledge and Kegan Paul.

Bevan, Hugh K. and Parry, Martin L. (1978) *Children Act 1975.* Butterworths.

Brown, Paul D. and Bloomfield, Terry (eds.) (1979) *Legality and Community.* Aberdeen People's Press.

Cawson, Pat and Martell M. (1979) *Children Referred to Closed Units.* DHSS

Carlen, Pat (1976) *Magistrates' Justice.* Martin Robertson.

Cawson, Pat and Martell J. (1979) *Children Referred to Closed Units.* DHSS Research Report No.5. HMSO.

Central Council for Education and Training in Social Work (1978) *Good Enough Parenting.* CCETSW.

Cornish, D.B. and Clarke, R.V.G. (1975) *Residential Treatment and Its Effects on Delinquency.* HMSO.

Crow, Iain *The Detention Centre Experiment.* (1979). NACRO.

Ditchfield, J.A. (1976) *Police Cautioning in England and Wales.* HMSO.

Fears, Denise (1977) 'Communication in English Juvenile Courts' *Sociological Review.* Vol.25, No.1.

Goldstein, Joseph (1978) 'Psychoanalysis and a Jurisprudence of Child Placement' *International Journal of Law and Psychiatry.* Vol.1, p.111.

Goldstein, Joseph, Freud, Anna and Solnit, Albert J. (1973) *Beyond the Best Interests of the Child.* Free Press.

Gostin, Larry O. (1975) *A Human Condition.* MIND.

Gostin, Larry O. (1979) 'The Merger of Incompetency and Certification', *International Journal of Law and Psychiatry,* Vol.2 (in press).

Hoghugi, Masud (1978) *Troubled and Troublesome: Coping with Severely Disordered Children.* Burnett Books.

Holman, Robert (1976) *Inequality in Child Care.* Child Poverty Action Group.

Jackson, Joseph, Booth, Margaret and Harris, Brian (eds.) (1977). *Clarke Hall and Morrison: Law Relation to Children and Young Persons.* Butterworths.

Little, A. (1962) 'Borstal Success and the Quality of Borstal Inmates' *British Journal of Criminology.*

Martin, F.M. and Murray, Kathleen (1976) *Children's Hearings.* Scottish Academic Press.

Millham, Spencer, Bullock, Roger and Cherrett, Paul (1975) *After Grace – Teeth.* Human Context.

Millham, Spencer *et al* (1978) *Locking Up Children.* Saxon House.

Morris, A.M. and Giller, H. (1978) 'The Juvenile Court – The Client's Perspective' *Criminal Law Review.* April 1978.

Morris, Allison M. (1978) 'Revolution in the Juvenile Court: The Juvenile Justice Standards Project' *Criminal Law Review.* September 1978.

Oswin, Maureen (1973) *The Empty Hours.* Pelican Books.

Oswin, Maureen (1978) *Children Living in Long-Stay Hospitals.* William Heinemann.

Page, Raissa and Clark, G.A. (eds.) (1977) *Who Cares? Young People in Care Speak Out.* National Children's Bureau.

Perry, F.G. (1975) *A Guide to the Preparation of Social Enquiry Reports.* Barry Rose.

Priestley, Philip, Fears, Denise and Fuller, Roger (1977) *Justice for Juveniles. The 1969 Children and Young Persons Act: A Case for Reform?* Routledge and Kegan Paul.

Prosser, T. (1977) 'Poverty, Ideology and Legality' *British Journal of Law and Society.* 4 39-60.

Reinach, E., Lovelock, R., Roberts, G. and Gude P. (1976) *First Year at Fairfield Lodge.* Portsmouth Polytechnic/Hampshire Social Services.

Rosenheim, Margaret K. (ed.) (1976) *Pursuing Justice for the Child.* University of Chicago Press.

Sinclair, I., Tizard, J. and Clarke, R., (eds.) (1975) *Varieties of Residential Experience.* Routledge and Kegan Paul.

Thorpe, D., Paley, J. and Green, G. (1979) 'The Making of a Delinquent' *Community Care.* 26 April 1979.

Thorpe, Jennifer (1979) *Social Enquiry Reports.* HMSO.

Tutt, Norman (1976) 'Recommittals of Juvenile Offenders' *British Journal of Criminology.* Vol.16, No.4.

Tutt, Norman (1977) *The Philosophy of Observation and Assessment.* Paper prepared for DHSS Seminar on Use and Development of O and A Centres for children.

Walter, J.A. (1978) *Sent Away: A Study of Young Offenders in Care.* Saxon House.

Zander, Michael (1975) 'What Happens to Young Offenders' *New Society* 24 July.

Other Publications

Behavioural Units (1978) DES.

Children and Young Persons Act (1969) HMSO.

Children in Trouble (1968). HMSO.

Children and Young Persons in Trouble (1977). NACRO.

Expenditure Committee Eleventh Report (1975) *The Children and Young Persons Act 1969.* HMSO.

Community Work and Caring for Children (1979) Report of the Harlesden Community Project Owen Wells.

Children in Care in England and Wales (1977). HMSO.

Special Educational Needs (1978) *Report of the Committee of Enquiry into the Education of Handcapped Children and Young People* (The Warnock Report). HMSO.

Report of the Interdepartmental Committee on the Business of Criminal Courts (1962) HMSO. Cmnd 1289. (The Streatfield Report).

Appendix

Legal Proceedings Which Lead to The Care or Custody of Children

In this section we set out in simplified form the main sections of the Acts under which a child or young person may be committed to the care, custody or detention of a local authority, or to borstal or to be detained in a place specified by the Secretary of State. As will be seen, there are six separate statutes under which a child may be committed to the care of a local authority, and orders under these statutes may be made in juvenile courts, magistrates courts, the County Court, the Crown Court and the Family Division of the High Court. As we have shown in our section on the legal representation of children, a child's right to separate representation varies from statute to statute, in some proceedings he has an absolute right to be represented, in others this is left to the discretion of the court. Furthermore, the nature of proceedings varies according to the different types of court involved in making care orders. What is more the different statutes and legal standards governing the committal of children to care are differently worded in different Acts. This complexity and confusion reflects the piecemeal fashion in which this legislation has been drawn up and implemented. As the editors of Clarke Hall and Morrison state in their preface to the ninth edition 'Clearly the law relating to children cannot be left in its present state, with its proliferation of categories and with so much that is enacted not yet in force' (Jackson *et al* 1977). As we have shown in our discussion, there is an urgent need for the laws concerning children to be consolidated and for the legal criteria governing the intervention by the law into the lives of children and their families to be clarified and codified in more specific and less ambiguous legal standards. We would, for example, favour the codifying in legal terms of such principles as the 'least restrictive setting' and the 'least detrimental available alternative' in legal proceedings concerned to establish the best interests of the child. The law should recognise that statutory agencies may be prone to actions in respect of children which are politically expedient rather than in a child's best interests. Equally, the law should recognise its limitations in supervising inter-personal relationships, and the doubtful validity of long-term predictions about the 'best interests of the child'.

Children and the law; proceedings leading to care or custody

Children Act 1948

Section 1. Duty of local authority to provide for orphans, deserted children, etc.

1. where it appears to a local authority that with respect to a child in their area appearing to be under the age of 17 —

   a. that he has neither parent nor guardian or has been and remains abandoned by his parents or guardian or is lost; or

   b. that his parents or guardian are, for the time being or permanently, prevented by reason of mental or bodily disease or infirmity or other incapacity or any other circumstances from providing for his proper accommodation maintenance and upbringing; and

   c. in either case that the intervention of the local authority under this section is necessary in the interests of the welfare of the child, it shall be the duty of the local authority to receive the child into care under this section.

2. where a local authority has received a child into their care under this section, it shall be subject to the provisions of this part of the Act, be their duty to keep the child in their care so long as the welfare of the child appears to them to require it and the child has not attained the age of eighteen.

3. nothing in this section shall authorise a local authority to keep a child in their care under this section if any parent or guardian desires to take over the care of the child, and the local authority shall, in all cases where it appears to them consistent with the welfare of the child so to do, endeavour to secure that the care of the child is taken over either—

   a. by a parent or guardian of his, or

   b. by a relative or friend of his being, where possible, a person of the same religious persuasion of the child or who gives an undertaking that the child will be brought up in that religious persuasion.

3a. Except in relation to an act done —

   a. with the consent of the local authority, or

   b. by a parent or guardian of the child who has given the local authority not less than 28 days notice of his intention to do it; subsection (8) penalty for taking away a child in care) of section 3 of this Act shall apply to a child in the care of a local authority under this section (notwithstanding that no resolution is in force under section 2 of this Act with respect to the child) if he has been in the care of that local authority throughout the preceding six months; and for the purpose of the application of paragraph (b) of that subsection, in such a case a parent or guardian of the child shall not be taken to have lawful authority to take him away.

3b. The Secretary of State may, by order of a draft which has been approved by each House of Parliament, amend subsection (3a) of this section by substituting a different period for the period of 28 days or of six months mentioned in that subsection (or the period which, by a previous order under this subsection, was substituted for that period).

Children are *received* into care by local authorities under section 1 Children Act 1948. Thus, it is generally regarded that a parent requests the local authority to receive his child into care, and provided that the child has not remained in care for a period of six months or more, that the parent can, on request, remove the child from the care of the local authority. If the child has been in care for more than six months, the parent must give 28 days notice of his intention to remove the child from care. However, it is possible in law for a local authority to prevent the child from being discharged from care by passing a resolution assuming the parental rights and powers in respect of that child. The House of Lords has ruled that a local authority may take parental rights and powers over a child who has been placed voluntarily in care if, despite the request of the parents, the local authority feels that the welfare of the child demands this. A local authority may also apply for a child to be made a ward of court if they feel that the welfare of the child would require that he should remain in care.

Children Act 1948
Section 2
Assumption by local authority of parental rights and duties

1. Subject to the provisions of this part of the Act, if it appears to a local authority in relation to any child who is in their care under the foregoing section —

   a. that his parents are dead and he has no guardian or custodian; or

   b. that a parent of his —

       i. has abandoned him; or

       ii. suffers from some permanent disability rendering him incapable of caring for the child; or

       iii. while not failing with sub-paragraph (ii) of this paragraph, suffers from a mental disorder (within the meaning of the Mental Health Act 1959), which renders him unfit to have the care of the child; or

       iv. is of such habits or mode of life as to be unfit to have the care of the child; or

       v. has so consistently failed without reasonable cause to discharge the obligations of a parent as to have the care of the child; or

   c. that a resolution under paragraph (b) of this subsection is in force in relation to one parent of the child who is, or is likely to become, a member of the household, comprising the child and other parent; or

   d. that throughout the three years preceding the passing of the resolution the child has been in the care of a local authority under the foregoing section, or partly in the care of a local authority and partly in the care of a voluntary organisation, the local authority may resolve that there shall vest in them the parental rights and duties with respect to that child, and if the rights and duties were vested in the parent on whose account the resolution was passed jointly with another person, they shall also be vested in the local authority jointly with that other person.

When a local authority decides to assume the parental rights and duties of a parent, they have a duty to inform that parent (if that parent's whereabouts are known) in writing, of their intentions of doing so. They are also bound to inform the parents of the grounds on which they propose to take the action and that the parent has a right, within 28 days, to serve, in writing, on the local authority, an objection to the assumption of their parental rights and duties in respect of the child, unless the parent has given written consent to the local authority to do so.

If the parent does serve on the local authority a written notice of their objection, the resolution lapses within 14 days of the notice being served. Where a local authority has received such a notice, they may, within 14 days, complain to a juvenile court. If they do this the resolution will remain in force until the court has made a determination on the complaint. The juvenile court can, if it is satisfied that the grounds on which the local authority proposed to assume the parent's rights and powers are made out, and that it is in the best interests of the child so to do, order that the parents objection should be overruled and that the parent's rights and powers should be vested in the local authority.

Conversely, if the juvenile court does not feel the local authority's grounds are made out, they must order that the parent's rights and powers remain vested with that parent.

Children and Young Persons Act 1969
Section 1.

Care proceedings in juvenile courts —

1. Any local authority, constable or authorised person who reasonably believes that there are grounds for making an order under this section in respect of a child or young person may, subject to section 2 (3) and 2 (8) of this Act, bring him before a juvenile court.

2. If the court before which a child or young person is brought under this section is of the opinion that any of the following conditions is satisfied with respect of him, that is to say —

   a. his proper development is being avoidably prevented or neglected or his health is being avoidably impaired or neglected or he is being ill treated; or

   b. it is probable that the condition set out in the preceding paragraph will be satisfied in his case, having regard to the fact that the court or another court has found that the condition is, or was, satisfied in the case of another child or young person who is, or was, a member of the household to which he belongs; or

   bb. it is probable that the conditions set out in paragraph (a) of this subsection will be satisfied in his case, having regard to the fact that a person who has been convicted of an offence mentioned in Schedule 1 to the Act of 1933 is, or may become, a member of the same household as the child; or.

   c. he is exposed to moral danger; or

d. he is beyond the control of his parent or guardian; or

e. he is of compulsory school age within the meaning of the Education Act 1944, and is not receiving efficient full-time education suitable to his age, ability and aptitude; or

f. he is guilty of an offence, excluding homicide, and also that he is in need of care and control which he is unlikely to receive unless the court makes an order under this section in respect of him, then, subject to the following provisions of this section and sections 2 and 3 of this Act, the court may, if it thinks fit, make such an order.

3. The order which a court may make under this section in respect of a child is —

a. an order requiring his parent or guardian to enter into a recognisance to take proper care of him and exercise proper control over him; or

b. a supervision order; or

c. a care order (other than an interim order); or

d. a hospital order within the meaning of Part V of the Mental Health Act 1959; or

e. a guardianship order within the meaning of that Act.

Children and Young Persons Act 1969
Section 7

7. Subject to the enactments requiring cases to be remitted to juvenile courts and to section 53 (i) of the Act of 1933 (which provides for the detention for certain grave crimes), where a child is found guilty of homicide or a young person is found guilty or any offence by or before any court, that court, or court to which his case is remitted, shall have power —

a. if the offence is punishable in the case of an adult with imprisonment, to make a care order (other than an interim order) in respect of him; or

b. to make a supervision order in respect of him; or

c. with the consent of his parent or guardian; to order the parent or guardian to enter into a recognisance to take proper care of him and exercise proper control over him.

Children and Young Persons Act 1969
Section 15
Variation and discharge of supervision orders —

1. If while a supervision order is in force in respect of a supervised person who has not attained the age of 18, it appears to a juvenile court, on the application of the supervisory or the supervised person, that it is appropriate to make an order under this subsection, the court may make an order discharging the supervision order or varying it by —

a. cancelling any requirements included in it in pursuance of section 12 or section 18 (2) of this Act; or

b. inserting in it (either in addition to, or in substitution for, any of its provisions) any provision which could have been included in the order if the court had then the power to make it and were exercising the power, and may, on discharging the supervision order, make a care order (other than an interim order) in respect of the supervised person.

Children and Young Persons Act 1969
Section 20

3. Subject to the provisions of the following section, a care order other than an interim order shall cease to have effect —

    a. if the person to whom it relates had attained the age of 16 when the order was originally made, when he attains the age of 19; and

    b. in any other case, when that person attains the age of 18.

4. A care order shall be sufficient authority for the detention by any local authority or constable of the person to whom the order relates until he is received into the care of the authority to whose care he is committed to care by the order.

Children and Young Persons Act 1969
Section 23
Remand to the care of local authorities, etc. —

1. Where a court — (a) remands or commits for trial a child charged with homicide; or (b) remands a young person charged with, or convicted of, one or more offences or commits him for trial for sentence, and he is not released on bail, then, subject to the following provisions of this section, the court shall commit him to the care of the local authority in whose area it appears to the court that he resides or that the offence, or one of the offences, was committed.

2. If the court aforesaid certifies that a young person is of so unruly a character that he cannot be committed to the care of the local authority under the preceding subsection, then if the court has been notified by the Secretary of State that a remand centre is available for the reception from the court of persons of his class or description, it shall commit him to a remand centre and, if it has not been notified, it shall commit him to a prison.

Children and Young Persons Act 1969
Section 28
Definition of child or young person in place of safety —

1. If, upon an application to a justice by any person for authority to detain a child or young person and take him to a place of safety, the justice is satisfied that the applicant has reasonable cause to believe that —

    a. any of the conditions set out in section 1 (2) (a) to (e) of this Act is satisfied in respect of a child or young person; or

    b. an appropriate court would find the condition set out in section 1 (2) (b) of this Act satisfied in respect of him; or

    c. the child or young person is about to leave the United Kingdom in contravention of section 25 of the Act of 1933 (which regulates the sending abroad of juvenile entertainers), the justice may grant the application; and the child or young person in respect of whom an authorisation is issued under the subsection may be detained in a place of safety by virtue of the authorisation for 28 days, or for such shorter period beginning with that date as may be specified in the authorisation.

2. Any constable may detain a child or young person as respects whom the constable has reasonable cause to believe that any of the conditions set out in section 1 (2) (a) to (d) of this Act is satisfied or that an appropriate court would find the condition set out in section 1 (2) (b) of this Act satisfied that an offence is being committed under section 10 (1) of the Act of 1933 (which penalises a vagrant who takes a child from place to place).

Children and Young Persons Act 1969
Section 30
Detention of young offenders in community homes —

1. The power to give directions under section 53 of the Act of 1933 (under which young offenders convicted on indictment of certain grave crimes may be detained in accordance with directions given by the Secretary of State) shall include power to direct detention by a local authority specified in the directions in a home so specified which is a community home provided by the authority or a controlled community home for the management, equipment and maintenance of which the authority are responsible; but a person shall not be liable to be detained in the manner provided by this section after he attains the age of nineteen.

2. It shall be the duty of the local authority specified in directions given in pursuance of this section to detain the person to whom the directions relate in the home specified in the directions subject to, and in accordance with, such instructions relating to him as the Secretary of State may give to the authority from time to time; and the authority shall be entitled to recover from the Secretary of State any expenses reasonably incurred by them in discharging that duty.

Children and Young Persons Act 1969
Section 31
Removal to borstal institutions of persons committed to the care of local authorities —

1. Where a person who has attained the age of fifteen is, for the time being, committed to the care of a local authority by a care order (other than an interim order) and accommodated in a community home and the local authority consider that he ought to be removed to a borstal institution under this section, they may, with the consent of the Secretary of State, bring him before a juvenile court.

2. If the court before which a person is brought in pursuance of this section is satisfied that his behaviour is such that it will be detrimental to the persons

accommodated there, the court may order him to be removed to a borstal institution.

(N.B. This section does not specify that the original care order should have been made under the offence conditions of section 1 of this Act. Therefore, this section makes it possible for a person not convicted of an offence to be committed for borstal training).

Children and Young Persons Act 1933

Section 53 Punishment of certain grave crimes —

1. A person convicted of an offence who appears to the court to have been under the age of 18 years at the time of the offence was committed shall not . be if he is convicted of murder, be sentenced to imprisonment for life nor shall sentence of death be pronounced on, or recorded against, any such person; but in leiu thereof the court shall (notwithstanding anything in this or any other Act) sentence him to be detained during Her Majesty's Pleasure; and if so sentenced he shall be liable to be detained in such a place and under such conditions as the Secretary of State may direct.

2. Where a child or young person is convicted on indictment of any offence punishable in the case of an adult with imprisonment for fourteen years or more, not being an offence the sentence for which is fixed by law, and the court is of opinion that none of the other methods in which the case may legally be dealt with is suitable, the court may sentence the offender to be detained for such period not exceeding the maximum term of imprisonment with which the offence is punishable in the case of an adult or may be specified in the sentence; and where such a sentence has been passed the child or young person shall, during that period, be liable to be detained in such place and under such conditions as the Secretary of State may direct.

Children Act 1975

Section 17 Care, etc., of child on refusal of an adoption order —

1. Where, on an application for an adoption order in relation to a child under the age of 16, the court refused to make the adoption order, then —

   a. if it appears to the court that there are exceptional circumstances making it desirable that the child should be under the supervision of an independent person, the court may order that the child shall be under the supervision of a specified local authority or under the supervision of a probation officer;

   b. if it appears to the court that there are exceptional circumstances making it impractical or undesirable for the child to be entrusted to either of the parents or to any other individual, the court may, by order, commit the child to the care of a specified local authority.

Section 36 Care, etc., of a child on revocation of custodianship order —

1. Before revoking a custodianship order the court shall ascertain who would

have legal custody of the child, if, on the revocation of the custodianship order, no further order were made under this section.

2. If the child would not be in the legal custody of any person, the court shall, if it revokes the custodianship order, commit the care of the child to a specified local authority.

3. If there is a person who would have legal custody of the child on revocation of the custodianship order, the court shall consider whether it is desirable in the interests of the welfare of the child for the child to be in the legal custody of that person and –

a. if the court is of the opinion that it would not be so desirable, it shall, on revoking the custodianship order, commit the care of the child to a specified local authority.

Care orders made in matrimonial proceedings

Matrimonial Proceedings (Magistrates Courts) Act 1960

Section 2 (1) (e) – if it appears to the court that there are exceptional circumstances making it impractical or undesirable for any such child as aforesaid to be entrusted in either of the parties or any other individual, a provision committing the care of a child to a specified local authority, being the local social services authority for the area in which the child was, in the opinion of the court, resident immediately before being so committed.

Matrimonial Causes Act 1973

Section 43 Power to commit child to care of local authority – (1) Where the court has jurisdiction by virtue of this Part of this Act to make an order for the custody of a child and it appears to the court that there are exceptional circumstances making it impracticable or undesirable for a child to be entrusted to either of the parties to the marriage or to any other individual, the court may if it thinks fit make an order committing the cre of the child to the council of a county other than ametropolitan county, or of a metropolitan district or London borough or the Common Council of the City of London (hereafter in this section referred to as 'the local authority'); and there Part II of the Children Act 1948 (which relates to the treatment of children in the care of a local authority) shall, subject to the provisions of this section, apply as if the child had been received by the local authority into their care under section 1 of that Act.

Guardianship Act 1973

Section 2 (2) (b) – if it appears to the court that there are exceptional circumstances making it impracticable or undesirable for the minor to be entrusted to either of the parents *or to any other individual,* the court may commit the care of a minor to a specified local authority.

Family Law Reform Act 1969

Section 7 Committal of wards of care to local authority and supervision of wards of court –

1. In this section 'the court' means any of the following courts in the exercise of its jurisdictions relating to the wardship of child, that is to say, the High Court, and 'ward of court' means a ward of the court in question.

2. Where it appears to the court that there are exceptional circumstances making it impracticable or undesirable for a ward of court to be, or to continue to be, under the care of either of his parents or any other individual the court may, if it thinks fit, make an order committing the care of the ward to a local authority.

Wardship

Jurisdiction in wardship is confined to the Family Division of the High Court. Wardship is the exercise by the court of its inherent jurisdiction derived from the ancient doctrine of *parens patrie,* the obligation of the state to protect the persons or property of its citizens, particularly those who may be unable to protect and promote their own interests, such as, for example, children or mentally handicapped persons. Thus wardship is not a jurisdiction derived from statute.

Any person having a proper interest in a child may apply for an order of wardship to the Family Division of the High Court. (See, for example, the case Re D *(A Minor) (Wardship: Sterilisation)* 1976 Fam 185 pp.192, 193; 1976 1 All E.R. 326 p.332, in which an educational psychologist applied to make an eleven year old mentally handicapped girl a ward to prevent her being sterilised.) As soon as the originating summons is issued the child becomes a ward, and remains a ward for twenty-one days, when, if an application for an appointment has not been made, the order lapses. However, once an application for a hearing has been made, a registrar of the Family Division may determine interlocutory matters such as, for example, parental access to a child in care.

The wardship jurisdiction of the High Court does not apply to children in care in respect of whom a resolution vesting the parental rights and duties in a local authority under the provisions of section 2 Children Act 1948, is in existence. Neither does this jurisdiction apply to a child who has been refused admission to the United Kingdom by the immigration authorities, or to a child whose parent claims diplomatic immunity. With these exceptions the wardship jurisdiction applies very widely to the care and affairs of children. In wardship proceedings rules of strict confidentiality apply. Thus it is unlawful to publish the identity of a ward or to publish details of his circumstances which may lead to his being identified. In 1978 a local authority applied for two children in their care to be made wards of court, specifically to prevent their parents appearing in a television programme concerned with children in care. Wardship can be used to prevent the discharge from care of children. MIND was involved in a case in which a local authority threatened to ward a child when his mother gave them the statutory 28 days notice of her intention to discharge the child from care. When, on the advice of her lawyer, she began wardship proceedings herself, the local authority discharged the child from care.

Legal Aid in Juvenile Proceedings

The following chart taken from the Legal Action Group *Bulletin*, August 1976, describes the present complex position in regard to legal aid in juvenile proceedings.

Nature of proceedings	Legislation	Court	Who is eligible for legal aid?	Power to grant legal aid	Civil or criminal legal aid
1. Local authority seeks to take over parental rights	s2 1948 Act	Juvenile	Parent, guardian, or person with custody of child	sch 1 para 3 (c) 1974 Act	Civil
2. Application to terminate local authority's "parental" rights	s4 1948 Act	Juvenile	..	..	..
3. Appeal against orders made or refused under (1) or (2) above	s58 1975 Act (not yet in force)	High	..	sch 1 para 1 1974 Act	..
4. Seeking order that local authority bring child before court as beyond control	s3 1963 Act	Juvenile	Parent or guardian	sch 1 para 3 (c) 1974 Act	..
5. Application for care order	s1 1969 Act	Juvenile	Child	s28 (3) 1974 Act	Criminal
6. Appeals against order (or finding) made under (5) above	s2 (12) (or s3 (8)) 1969 Act	Crown	Child	s28 (3) 1974 Act	..
7. Varying or discharging supervision order	s15 (1) 1969 Act	Juvenile	..	s28 (3) 1974 Act	..
8. Appeals against order made under (7) above	s16 (8) 1969 Act	Crown	..	s28 (6) 1974 Act	..
9. Application to extend care order beyond 18 years of age	s21 (1) 1969 Act	Juvenile	..	s28 (3) 1974 Act	..
10. Application by local authority or child to discharge care order, and if appropriate substitute supervision order	s21 (2) 1969 Act	Juvenile	..	..	..
11. Appeals against order made under (9) or (10) above	s21 (4) 1969 Act	Crown	..	s28 (6) 1974 Act	..
12. Application to change care order to borstal	s31 (1) 1969 Act	Juvenile	..	s28 (3) 1964 Act	..
13. Appeal against order made under (12) above	s31 (6) 1969 Act	Crown	..	s28 (6) 1974 Act	..
14. Application to discharge an interim care order	s22 (4) 1969 Act	High	..	sch 1 para 1 1974 Act	Civil
15. Representation (of parent) in proceedings under (5), (6), (7), (8), (9), (10), (11) above	s64 1975 Act (not yet in force)	See (5), (6), (7), (8), (9), (10), (11) above	Parent	s65 1975	Criminal

Key:
1948 Act Children Act 1948 Act
1963 Act Children and Young Persons Act 1963
1969 Act Children and Young Persons Act 1969
1974 Act Legal Aid Act 1974
1975 Act Children Act 1975